All you ever wanted to know about Korea
This is Korea

All you ever wanted to know about Korea

This is Korea

CHOI Jung-wha & LIM Hyang-ok

Hollym

All you ever wanted to know about Korea
This is Korea (New Edition)

Copyright © 2011 by CHOI Jung-wha & LIM Hyang-ok

All rights reserved.
No part of this book may be used in any form,
without written permission from the author and the publisher.

This book was originally published by NEWRUN,
an Imprint of Woongjin Think Big Co., Ltd., Seoul, Korea.

First published in 2010
by Hollym International Corp, USA
Phone 908 353 1655   Fax 908 353 0255
http://www.hollym.com   e-Mail contact@hollym.com

Hollym

Published simultaneously in Korea
by Hollym Corp., Publishers, Seoul, Korea
Phone +82 2 734 5087   Fax +82 2 730 5149
http://www.hollym.co.kr   e-Mail info@hollym.co.kr

ISBN: 978-1-56591-299-1
Library of Congress Control Number: 2010941062

Printed in Korea

* Romanization of Korean names in this book follows the Romanization System used by the Korean Government since 2000.

PREFACE

Walk into any bookstore in downtown Seoul and you are sure to find numerous books about Korea—some about Korea in general, others about specific aspects of Korean culture such as its food (kimchi is the favorite), temples or even *hanbok*.

So, why another book about Korea? We felt that books out on the market offer readers, especially visitors, an overly sanitized version of Korea. They do not approach Korea from the perspective of the foreigner who really wants to know what makes Korea tick. Many foreigners say that Korea is not at all what they expected. In many ways it is overshadowed by its two neighbors in size by China and in economic size by Japan, and therefore is relatively unknown. And what little is known is often inaccurate or just a sliver of the whole. It is our hope that this book will give a more well-rounded view of our country.

We worked to make the style as reader-friendly as possible, as if your Korean friend were explaining to you what Korea is really like—warts and all! We hope that as you read this book, you will be drawn by the contrasts between tradition and modernity, and learn to like and even love Korea as we do.

December, 2010
CHOI Jung-wha & LIM Hyang-ok

Contents

PART 1
Basic Facts about Korea
Where Is Korea? 015
A Country Blessed with Four Distinct Seasons 016
Symbols of Korea 017
The World's Most Scientific Writing System, Hangeul 018
And Then Korea Was Created 022
5,000 Years of History 024
Major Holidays 026
Warm-hearted but Busy Koreans 029

PART 2
The Life of Koreans
: A tug-of-war between Tradition and Modernity
Proper Manners in General 035
Not Calling Each Other's Names, Human Relationships 038
The Art of the Gentle Refusal 040
Take off Your Shoes! 041
The Best of Both Worlds, Getting Married 044
Death, C'est la vie 050
The Korean Way, Counting Your Age 054
Counting Moons, The Lunar Calendar 056
The Korean Zodiac 059
Counseling Korean Style, The Fortune Telling 072

Colors, Striking a Balance	074
Using Seals Instead of Signatures	077
Lucky Numbers Unlucky Numbers	078
Bringing the Right Gift	080
Spoons and Chopsticks	081
Korean Tales	082

PART 3
A Glimpse of Korean Kitchen
: from the Special Occasion to the Routine

The Source of Korean's Energy, Rice	089
One of the World's Most Healthful Foods, Kimchi	091
The Older the Better, Fermented Foods	096
The Favorite Airline Food, *Bibimbap*	098
The Favorite of Foreign Visitors, Bulgogi	100
The Key Is in the Stew	101
When You Need a Boost of Energy, *Samgyetang*	102
Korean's Favorite Noodles, *Japchae*	104
Something to Snack on	106
Bread is to the West What *Tteok* is to Korea	107
Straight from the Ground to Medicine Cabinet, Korean Ginseng	108
Enjoy a Cup of Tea!	109
Korean Alcohol, *Soju* and *Makgeolli*	111
Table Manners	112

PART 4
A Guide for Armchair Travelers
: Spots and Places

Breathing Life into Seoul, The Hangang River	117
Royal Palaces	118
Catching a Glimpse of Life in the Past, Traditional Villages	120
Housing a Feat in Printing History, Haeinsa Temple	124
Korean Buddhism and Buddhist Temples	126
See the Seas Divide, Jindo Island	129
The Cradle of Ancient Civilization, Gyeongju	132
The Beautiful Southern Island, Jejudo	136
Traditional Street, Insa-dong	140
A Traditional Village Nestled in the City, Bukchon	142
A Bustling Business Area, COEX	145
Need Downtime? Cheonggyecheon Stream Is the Place to Go	146
The Ugly Duckling Turns into a Swan, Seonyudo Park	148
A Little Bit of the World in Seoul, Itaewon	149
Full of Life and Energy, Namdaemun & Dongdaemun Markets	150
Home of Seagulls, Dokdo Islets	151
Experience First-hand the Division of a Country, Panmunjeom	152
The Beauty of 12,000 Mountain Peaks, Geumgangsan	154

What They Are Saying About *This is Korea*...

Alan Timblick, Senior Advisor, Invest Korea, KOTRA

Having lived in Korea for over 20 years now, I have come to love this country. However, I feel that it is the best kept secret of the Orient. Not many people know Korea and even less, the Korean people. Once you meet them and get to know them, they become your friends for life. Though there are many books that introduce Korea to foreigners, this book looks at Korea from the perspective of the foreigner and explains why things are different in Korea.

Alan Cassels, CEO of DHL Korea

When I first came to Korea, I was the first non-Korean CEO to be appointed to DHL Korea and was unsure what to expect. If I had read this book before coming to Korea I would certainly have been better prepared. I've lived in many Asian countries but each country is different and this book gives the reader a true understanding of the Korean psyche. I would recommend it to both the casual visitor as well as an expat posted to this country.

PART 5
Korean Art
: the Beauty of Simplicity

A Reflection of Korean Philosophy, *Hanok*	159
Nature Untouched, Korean Gardens	162
Beauty in the Lines, *Hanbok*	164
Visual Art Expressed Through Lines	166
Where Art and Practicality Meet, Pottery	167
Traditional Korean Music	168
Korean Musicals in Disguise, Masks and Mask Dances	172
Grace in Motion, Traditional Dance	174
Forget Your Troubles in Traditional Games	176
The Way of Fist and Feet, Taekwondo	179

PART 6
Meet Korea Today
: Everything Changes Except Change Itself

At the Cutting Edge, IT Korea	185
Korean Culture Sweeping Across Asia, *Hallyu*	188
Fast and Efficient Transportation System	191
Korea's Room Culture	192
A World Inside the Internet, Cyworld	194
Early Adopters	196
B-boys on Top of the World	197

Anna Fifield, Financial Times Correspondent

Though I've been in Korea for two years now and have picked up a little of the language, I still feel that I have a lot to learn about this fascinating country. After reading this book, I have come to see a new depth in the culture and tradition of Korea. It would have helped enormously if I had had this book when I first came to this country, but even now it is not too late!

H.E. Jane Coombs, New Zealand Ambassador to Korea

When I came to Korea, I had very high expectations and I can honestly say that the people, the culture, the food — everything about this country has exceeded my expectations. I think that Korea is the best kept secret of Asia, but the secret is about to be revealed in this book. The two authors of this book reveal Korea to the rest of the world in a way that it has never been portrayed before.

PART 1
Basic Facts about Korea

Where Is Korea?

When asked to name a country in Asia, most people around the world would probably say China or Japan. But nestled between China and Japan is Korea, a peninsula shaped like a tiger, which has historically acted as a bridge between the two countries, and thus, has also been on the receiving end of numerous invasions. Koreans, peace-loving people that they are, take pride in the fact that they have never invaded another country.

The Korean peninsula is long at the top and bottom. The population of North and South Korea is approximately 73 million people. The peninsula faces China and Russia to the north, with the other three sides of the peninsula surrounded by the sea. South Korea has about 3,200 islands and islets. The land area of North and South Korea combined is 220,000 square kilometers, but there are so many steep mountains that the habitable area is relatively small.

Korea is at the same latitude as Madrid, Athens, San Francisco and New York. The farthest country from it is Argentina and the closest country is China.

[wichi] 위치

A Country Blessed with
Four Distinct Seasons

An oft-heard comment is that Korea has four distinct seasons.

Winter is cold with lots of snow, even in the large cities. Thankfully, traditionally there is the "three cold, four warm" cycle, which means that for every three very cold days, there are four slightly warmer days; spring is glorious with all the flowers and trees in full bloom; summer usually starts out with the monsoon (rainy season)—which seems to get shorter every year—and then is followed by sometimes unbearable humidity. In fall, all the trees change color to create a breathtaking splash of color.

Having four distinct seasons allows sport fanatics to enjoy a variety of sports befitting each season. Skiing, but more recently snowboarding, in the winter, and water sports in the summer.

Thanks to its mountainous terrain, Koreans love to go hiking, something that is all the more pleasurable because the mountains take on a different appearance depending on the season. In the spring, they become a lush green, while in the autumn, when the leaves turn color, the mountainsides seem to be ablaze.

[gyejeol]

Symbols of Korea

There are several symbols of Korea to which Koreans are particularly partial. One is the Rose of Sharon, the national flower of Korea, and another is the national anthem that all children learn in kindergarten, Aegukga 애국가. The national flag, Taegeukgi 태극기 is another special symbol. The *yin-yang* symbol in the middle of the flag is a motif often found in Asian culture and signifies opposites—man and woman, day and night, black and white, etc. The lines in the four corners represent the sky, earth, sun and moon.

The Korean currency is won 원. It comes in denominations of 50,000 won, 10,000 won, 5,000 won and 1,000 won bills, plus 500 won, 100 won, 50 won and 10 won coins. Don't be surprised with so many zeroes on the bills. One thousand won is rough equivalent to one US dollar. Also, don't be scared to use your credit card at stores across the country, as almost all of them accept all major credit cards.

How is Korea viewed by the outside world?

According to a survey conducted by the Corea Image Communication Institute in 2003, Korea's external image is that of a divided country (72%), a traditional culture (61%), a country of rapid economic growth (58%), the nation that hosted the World Cup (41%) and a country with traffic congestion (29%). Other external images included that of a vibrant, attractive and polite country.

[sangjingmul]

The World's Most Scientific Writing System
Hangeul

For Westerners, it is probably taken for granted that language is based on an alphabet and that words are formed by mixing and matching those consonants and vowels. However, the Chinese language does not have an alphabet. There is a Chinese character for each word. Needless to say, learning the language is very difficult.

Before the mid 15th century, male Korean aristocrats, *yangban*양반, learned Chinese, much like Latin was long taught as a classic written script in Europe. However, in the mid-15th century, King Sejong the Great세종대왕 commissioned a team of scholars to create an alphabet so that the masses could also read and write. This endeavor was conducted in secret because if word had gotten out, it would have met with great resistance from the elite. Luckily for us, King Sejong and his team succeeded in creating what is lauded today as being an extremely scientific form of writing. In fact, there is no other nation in the world that can pinpoint exactly when, where, why and by whom their writing system was developed or invented.

Hangeul한글, the Korean writing system, has been praised around the world for its simplicity and logic:

> "Hangeul, the alphabet used in Korea, is the world's most rational writing system. It is original and efficient, thanks to the scientific combination of the letters."
>
> _ Jared Diamond, June 1994, 《Discovery》

[han-geul]

"Hangeul is the simplest and best writing system in the world."
_Pearl Buck, author of *The Good Earth*

Successive kings did not always welcome the new alphabet and so it had its ups and downs. But in the late 19th century, it was used as a symbol by reformists. There is still an undercurrent of influence of the Chinese language on Korean. At times Chinese characters will be mixed in with Korean. At other times, a word might be written in hangeul as a transcription of the Chinese character. Sometimes, Asians who still use Chinese characters—the Chinese, Japanese and Koreans—can communicate with each other by writing down the Chinese characters which are pronounced differently in each language, but which usually retain the same meaning. It is also said that the Korean language has maintained the purity of the original Chinese characters, while Chinese has simplified most of them.

Hunmin jeongeum 훈민정음
Inscribed in the UNESCO Memory of the World Register on October 1, 1997, *Hunmin jeongeum* means "the right sounds to teach the people."
  Each year, UNESCO awards the King Sejong Literacy Prize (*Sejong daewangsang* 세종대왕상) in recognition of worthwhile contributions to fight illiteracy.

Hangeul Day 한글날
Hangeul Day was celebrated as a national holiday on October 9th of each year from 1946 to 1990. Many believe that in view of the importance of hangeul, the national holiday should be revived.

A 10-minute Lesson in Hangeul

Jung In-ji 정인지, one of the scholars of the Hall of Worthies who was entrusted with the task of developing hangeul, said, "It should take less than a morning for a wise person to learn, but even a dim-witted person can learn it in 10 days."

Korean Alphabet

Consonants

LETTER	CALLED		PRONOUNCED
ㄱ	giyeok	기역	g, k
ㄴ	nieun	니은	n
ㄷ	digeut	디귿	d
ㄹ	rieul	리을	r, l
ㅁ	mieum	미음	m
ㅂ	bieup	비읍	b
ㅅ	siot	시옷	s
ㅇ	ieung	이응	ng※
ㅈ	jieut	지읒	j
ㅊ	chieut	치읓	ch
ㅋ	kieuk	키읔	k
ㅌ	tieut	티읕	t
ㅍ	pieup	피읖	p
ㅎ	hieut	히읗	h
ㄲ	ssanggiyeok	쌍기역	kk
ㄸ	ssangdigeut	쌍디귿	tt
ㅃ	ssangbieup	쌍비읍	pp
ㅆ	ssangsiot	쌍시옷	ss
ㅉ	ssangjieut	쌍지읒	jj

※ silent at the beginning of a word

Vowels

LETTER	CALLED & PRONOUNCED	
ㅏ	a	아
ㅑ	ya	야
ㅓ	eo	어
ㅕ	yeo	여
ㅗ	o	오
ㅛ	yo	요
ㅜ	u	우
ㅠ	yu	유
ㅡ	eu	으
ㅣ	i	이
ㅐ	ae	애
ㅒ	yae	얘
ㅔ	e	에
ㅖ	ye	예
ㅘ	wa	와
ㅙ	wae	왜
ㅚ	oe	외
ㅝ	wo	워
ㅞ	we	웨
ㅟ	wi	위
ㅢ	ui	의

So let's give it a try:
Say your name is 'Betty' → 베티, 'Richard' → 리차드.
Have a go at it!

Survival Korean

These are several basic phrases that could come in handy for anyone visiting Korea. Koreans will appreciate the friendly gesture as well as your efforts to communicate with them in their own language.

- *ne/eung* 네/응. Yes.
- *aniyo* 아니요. No.
- *annyeonghaseyo* 안녕하세요? Good morning; Good afternoon; Good evening (greetings used when first seeing someone).
- *annyeonghi gyeseyo* 안녕히 계세요. Good-bye (when you're leaving).
- *annyeonghi gaseyo* 안녕히 가세요. Good-bye (when others are leaving).
- *gamsahamnida* 감사합니다. Thank you.
- *saranghaeyo* 사랑해요. I love you.
- *ppalli ppalli* 빨리빨리. Hurry; Quickly.
- *hwajangsiri eodi isseoyo* 화장실이 어디 있어요? Where is the restroom?
- *mannaseo bangapseumnida* 만나서 반갑습니다. Pleased to meet you.
- *mianhamnida* 미안합니다. I'm sorry.
- *je ireumeun piteoimnida* 제 이름은 피터입니다. My name is Peter.

And Then
Korea Was Created

As with many other countries, Korea also has a legend about its creation. This legend reflects many beliefs and philosophies that underpin the Korean mentality. National Foundation Day, celebrated on October 3, commemorates this legend.

The story goes that the heavens were ruled by King Hwanin 환인 who had a son named Hwanung 환웅. The son asked his father for permission to go down to earth so that he could help humans. His wish was granted and he was sent down to the most important land—what is now known as Korea. One day, a tiger and bear came to him, beseeching him to make them humans. He dissuaded them by telling them that it required enormous patience. The two would not be discouraged. Finally, he told them to eat 20 cloves of garlic and mugwort he would give them and to enter a cave and pray to the gods. They ate the garlic and mugwort and prayed to the gods. After a few days, however, the tiger was unable to bear his hunger pains and fled from the cave. The bear, however, patiently withstood the hardships and after 100 days was transformed into a beautiful woman. Hwanung named her Ungnyeo 웅녀 and married her. They in turn had a son, Dangun 단군, beloved as the first ancestor of the Korean people. Dangun founded the land known as Ancient Joseon 고조선 in 2333 BC, marking the beginning of Korea's ancient calendric system.

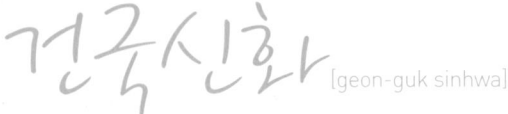
[geon-guk sinhwa]

Although most countries throughout the world follow the Gregorian (Christian) calendar, Koreans also recognize their own system (accordingly, 2010 is 4343). October 3 is National Foundation Day, the day that Dangun established Korea and therefore is a national holiday.

5,000 Years of History

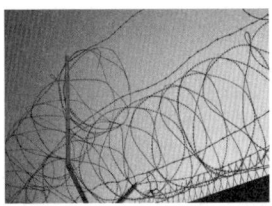

Despite the fact that Korea was subjected to numerous foreign invasions, it was able to maintain its national identity and language. However, in contemporary history, the country ended up being divided in two due to outside forces. Following World War II, the Korean peninsula was caught in a tug-of-war between superpowers trying to fight out their ideological differences. The result was a division between the South, which advocated capitalism, and the North, which advocated communism. Consequently, a civil war broke out between the two sides, which ended in an armistice. Afterwards, a military dictatorship took over in the South, while in the communist North, a hereditary dictatorship gained power. The two sides are the last remnants of the Cold War. As such, innumerable families have been separated by this artificial division and forced to live for more than five decades without any news of their loved ones.

In the 1980s, when South Korea finally achieved its long-held dream of democratization, the first signs of a Cold War thaw on the Korean peninsula appeared. Efforts to improve North-South relations included President Kim Dae-jung 김대중's Sunshine Policy as well as the Mt. Geumgangsan 금강산 tours, which allow South Koreans to visit those beautiful mountains in the North.

[yeoksa]

Another famous overture was made by the wealthy chairman of a large conglomerate in South Korea. Decades before, he had left his hometown in the North, taking with him a cow. To show his gratitude, in 1998 he arranged for 1,001 cows to be herded across the border to Pyeongyang 평양, the capital city of North Korea.

Such policies are sometimes successful, while at other times they are not. This can lead to tension and conflict between the two sides. However, the South will not give up its efforts to embrace the North as "part of the family."

A history of division and unity

The Korean people have lived through a history of division and unity. The peninsula has been divided into smaller states and then been reunited by whoever was in power. The major kingdoms of the past were Goguryeo 고구려, Baekje 백제 and Silla 신라, which were then united into the Unified Silla Kingdom. This was later followed by the Goryeo 고려 Dynasty and then the Joseon 조선 Dynasty. The Joseon Dynasty, which lasted for 500 years (until the Japanese invasion) was the last unified kingdom.

Major Holidays

Koreans are world-renowned for being diligent and hard-working. In fact, in the 1960s numerous Korean nurses went to Germany to fill the labor shortage of nurses in that country. In the process, they helped their home country by sending large portions of their earnings back to Korea. In the 1970s it was the men's turn. They went to the Middle East during the construction boom there, working in dire conditions to help their families back home. They scrimped and saved, forfeiting holidays and working overtime in order to earn a little more. It was thanks to them, in large part, that Korea was able to bring about an economic miracle. It's not if you're going, but where you're going, and oftentimes, Koreans enjoy going abroad. Nevertheless, vacations are still short compared to European standards, rarely lasting more than a week.

There are two major holidays in Korea, one is Lunar New Year's Day, Seollal 설날, and the other Korean Thanksgiving, Chuseok 추석. Both are determined by the lunar calendar; New Year's Day is on January 1 while Chuseok is on August 15. While 48.1% (as of 2005) of the Korean population resides in metropolitan areas, the majority has roots in the provinces. Hence, during the two holidays, there is a major exodus and Seoul becomes almost completely deserted like Rome in August 15.

Many Stores and restaurants close during the two holidsys and people enjoy a family reunion.

There are several rituals that occur during these two holidays. First and

[myeongjeol]

foremost is food. Since all family members and extended family get together at these times of the year, this naturally means feeding them all. So part of the ritual consists of conducting *charye*차례 which is a rite to honor one's ancestors. This entails great amounts of food. A table is laden with meat, fish, fruit, assorted vegetables, *tteok*떡 (rice cakes), chestnuts, dates and dried persimmons, with variations depending on the region and family traditions. Incense and candles are burned and the men bow several times. After the formalities are over, the family digs in and everyone eats to their heart's content. In the past, because so many Koreans were poor, this was one of the rare occasions when one's ancestors were able to eat until they were full. The most important dish at Lunar New Year's Day is *tteokguk*떡국 (rice cake soup). In the old days, white rice was expensive and hard to get, so it was not eaten very often. On Lunar New Year's Day, though, it was a must. In fact, there is a Korean saying that you haven't aged a year until you've had New Year's *tteokguk*.

Lunar New Year's Day was also a time to buy new clothes. Today it is also one of the few occasions people wear *hanbok*한복. Clad in their new clothes, the children bow deeply to their parents and elders, *sebae*세배, often wishing them good health and longevity. In return, young people are given pocket money, *sebaetdon*세뱃돈. The day is also for the games that Koreans love to play. It's not only a time for social interaction, but friendly competition as well. Family and relatives greet each other heartily and then settle down for some serious fun. The games more often enjoyed are *yunnori*윷놀이 (four wooden blocks game), *hwatu*화투 (flower cards), and *baduk*바둑

(go). In order to add a little bit of excitement to the game, many people often place bets. Children usually sit next to the adults and get as excited as the adults because they are given pocket money from the winnings. For Chuseok, *charye* is held once again, but without *tteokguk*. Also, *sebae* is not performed and *yunnori* is not played at this time of year. Again, new clothes are bought for everybody. It is customary to bring gifts when one goes home.

Yunnori

This is a game that is enjoyed by young and old alike. The "die" consist of two pieces of wood which are about 17cm long, and are cut in half so that they are smooth on one side and round on the other. The playing board is diamond shaped and each team has four pawns (in Korean, *mal*말, or "horses") and the object of the game is to get all your pawns home as quickly as possible.

The fun of the game is that you can tag another horse out if you land on it. The *yut*윷 (sticks) are thrown high up in the air to get the best result. If one die is over (flat side up), it is called *do*도; two, *gae*개; and three, *geol*걸. All sticks over is called *yut*윷, whereas all sticks up (round side up) is called *mo*모.

Hwatu

The perennial favorite of Koreans on any occasion is *hwatu*, literally meaning "flower battle." Hwatu is the name of the 48 cards, four cards for each month. The name of the game is "go-stop" because once you reach the minimum three points, you can decide whether you want to "go" (that is, continue and earn more points) or "stop" and simply win that hand. Among friends and family, there is a little gambling in order to add spice to the game. If you're bored, you can even try the Internet and join in on a game with others who are online.

Warm-hearted but Busy Koreans

Koreans use certain words to describe themselves. For example, Koreans are said to have a lot of *jeong*정. This is a difficult word to translate: affection, sympathy, compassion, love—the list goes on, but it is difficult to pin down. Perhaps the English idiom "to grow on someone" is the closest approximation of *jeong*. Some actions might be motivated solely by *jeong*.

Sometimes the warmth and hospitality of Korean people can be masked by their shyness when meeting foreign visitors. Tamy Overby, Vice President of the American Chamber of Commerce in Korea once related this story: "In 1988 when I first came to Korea, I went to Mt. Odaesan 오대산 with a friend. We got lost, but found a *yeogwan*여관 (inn) to stay at. We spent a comfortable night at the inn and the next morning, when we tried to pay for our keep, the innkeeper refused to accept our payment. He insisted that we had not slept in the *yeogwan* but that they had let us stay in the main bedroom because we were foreigners who had lost their way. This is unimaginable in the States. The people in Korea are so warm and so beautiful. How could I not like this country?"

Koreans also say that they are a people that have a lot of *han*한, which, again, is difficult to translate. A deep sadness, grief and sorrow mixed with a tinge of bitterness is one way of describing it. The accumulation of *han* is often attributed to the fact that Koreans have undergone so many foreign invasions and hardships over the years.

It is said that a feeling of profound sadness known as *han* lives in the heart of every Korean. Sometimes on the news or elsewhere bereaved relatives can be seen wailing uncontrollably for their lost loved ones. Such a family tragedy releases the suppressed *han*, which spills over in a flood of emotions. The lyrics and melodies of old Korean folk songs often reflect this deep emotion.

When describing Koreans, the most oft-used terms are "diligent," "always in a rush," "hot-tempered" and "*ppalli ppalli* 빨리빨리," or "rush-rush," qualities that have in one way or another contributed to the dramatic economic growth during the past five decades.

Koreans work hard but they also play hard. From ancient times, Koreans enjoyed wine, song and dance. It is considered a virtue to be modest, so under ordinary circumstances, should you ask a Korean to sing or dance, they will be reticent and act shy. But with a few drinks, the inhibitions melt away and they become boisterous and outgoing, belting out song after song. In fact, it is not unusual to see tipsy men (more often, men than women) singing or simply walking very unsteadily in the wee evening hours. It is a way for them to relieve the stress accumulated during the day.

Ppalli ppalli is one of the first Korean words that foreigners learn when they come to Korea. At lunch time, if you go to any restaurant around an office building and listen very carefully to how people order, it is very often, "*Seolleongtang han geureut ppalli juseyo*설렁탕 한 그릇 빨리 주세요," or "Please give me a bowl of *seolleongtang*설렁탕 quickly!" And within five minutes, they will be served.

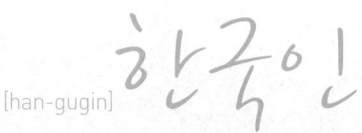

[han-gugin]

PART 2

The Life of Koreans
: A tug-of-war between Tradition and Modernity

Proper Manners in General

Showing proper manners to elders

It is sometimes said that Koreans are more Confucian than the Chinese. Following Confucian precepts, Korean social relationships are centered on five duties and obligations. The first relationship is between the father and son; the second, between ruler and subject; third, between husband and wife; fourth, between adult and child; and fifth, between friends. Almost every relationship, except that between friends, is based on the idea that one person has a higher status or vertical relationship. The person of lower status is duty-bound to respect and obey, while the one of higher status is supposed to look after and protect the other. This concept of protecting and being protected is so thoroughly ingrained in Korean society that it extends beyond families to graduates from the same university and people from the same hometown or region.

It used to be that everybody living in a village knew everybody else and therefore all elders were treated with the same respect offered to one's parents. However, as Korea becomes more Westernized and urbanized, these old traditions are fading quickly.

How should you treat an adult?
- Regardless of the number of times that you meet them in one day, remember to greet them with respect.
- If an adult doesn't remember you, remind him/her of who you are.

[yejeol] 예기절

- Ask about their recent news.
- Do not stay long when you visit a home of elders.
- Unless it is an emergency, do not overtake an elder when walking.
- Do not whistle in front of an elder.
- Do not boast about your house or wealth.
- Wait for the oldest person to begin eating first. Also, pace yourself so that you don't finish before he/she does.
- Do not smoke in front of a person of higher status.
- Do not drink in front of a higher-status person. If you must, turn your head to one side as a sign of respect.

Interpersonal manners

Though Korean children are taught basic manners at home, they are also taught in school with the aid of etiquette textbooks. Heavily influenced by Confucian philosophy, parents teach their children how to show respect to elders, and how to speak properly—using the correct terms of address and table manners. Greetings are an important part of overall good manners and reflect good upbringing. The greatest praise one can receive from an adult is, "That boy/girl really knows how to greet properly!" The proper greeting to one's elders and teachers is considered to be a reflection of good manners. Good manners include table manners. For example, when dining with elders, you wait until they start using their utensils before lifting yours.

Here are just a few general tips to interpersonal manners:
- Respect your elders by bowing first and using polite words/expressions.

- Bow to someone you are being introduced to.
- Bow to the person you want to greet or thank.
- Do not offer a hand to shake if the person is older.
- Do not talk loudly in public places.
- Do not shake your legs when seated on a chair or on the floor.
- Do not point at someone.
- Give up your seat on the bus or subway for an elder.
- When sitting on the floor, keep your legs folded, not stretched toward any adults.
- Cover your mouth when coughing, sneezing or laughing.
- Do not cut in line.
- When on the phone, do not hang up before the other does.
- Say "Good morning" and "Good night" to your parents.
- Say "Welcome home" when your parents return home.
- On your birthday, invite friends and family members for a nice meal.

Getting a load off your back
If you're on a crowded bus or subway and a seated passenger suddenly grabs your heavy bag, don't be alarmed and don't think that they're trying to steal your bag. It is more likely that the person sitting down just wants to relieve you of your burden since they are sitting down. This is a courtesy that is extended mostly to students, since their bookbags are often heavy and they are usually very tired from all the studying they do. The country as a whole pitches in to help students!

Not Calling Each Other's Names
Human Relationships

In Korea being senior or junior to someone has a special meaning. This could be at school—upper-classman and lower-classman—but also at work. If somebody joined the company before you, he/she would be your senior. Unlike Western societies, where relationships tend to be more horizontal, relationships in Korea tend to be vertical. The senior member, as such, will take care of the junior member, much like an older brother would take care of a younger one, while the junior member will reciprocate by respecting his/her senior.

In Korea, you can go through life barely hearing the sound of your own name. One of the reasons is that there are so many different appellations that you can go without the use of proper names. In the US, if you meet somebody for the first time, they will naturally say something like, "Call me Bill." But in Korea, since relationships are vertical, this would never happen. Right away, you would know to call them by their title—teacher, director, manager, or president, for example—or if they do not have a formal title, *ajumma* 아줌마 if she's female, or *ajeossi* 아저씨 if he's male. *Ajumma* actually means "aunt" and *ajeossi* means "uncle" which is an offshoot of the fact that all of society is actually supposed to be one happy family. Another quirk of the language is that instead of saying "my" house or even "my" husband, in Korean, you would say "our" house and "our" husband—even though we are monogamous!

호칭 [hoching]

However, *ajumma* and *ajeossi* have taken on a slightly pejorative connotation and therefore are used for cleaning ladies and taxi drivers or concierges. Instead, you might hear *eonni* 언니 being used by a girl to an older sister; a boy would call an older girl *nuna* 누나. Sometimes you might even hear a salesperson calling a client *eonni*, probably to make her feel younger. Men will sometimes call a waitress *eonni* as well.

Names that Koreans call each other
- Girl to older girl, *eonni* 언니
- Girl to older boy, *oppa* 오빠
- Boy to older girl, *nuna* 누나
- Boy to older boy, *hyeong* 형

The Art of
the Gentle Refusal

Traditionally, it is said that even if you agree with a proposal, it is proper to refuse three times. So, even if your counterpart says no, it may not mean no. If taken too literally, then your counterpart may be surprised that it is taken at face value. In general, even when a proposal is to a Korean's disadvantage, he/she will not refuse outright, and even when it is to their advantage, they will, because of face, gently refuse. It was not considered proper to express one's likes or dislikes overtly and even when there was something lacking, it was considered proper to overlook it or else lose face.

So how many times are you supposed to make the offer? Well, there's no fixed number. Often you just have to play it by ear. However, a word of caution: even if you do not drink, you should not refuse the first glass. It may be considered rude.

Saving face
As in many other Asian cultures, the concept of face is very important. One of the worst things that can happen to you is to lose face. And one of the manifestations of face is one's outward appearance, which is why Koreans are so preoccupied about their looks. In fact, Westerners are surprised to see so many large mirrors hanging in elevators, staircases or building walls. It's just that Koreans want to make sure that they look right when they meet other people. The intangible side of this is status-consciousness. Koreans are easily impressed by those who hold a higher position in society.

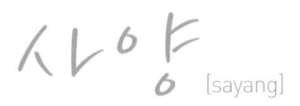

사양 [sayang]

Take off Your Shoes!

Japan has a marine climate and high humidity. Consequently, the Japanese bathe often and use *tatami* mats which are not easily affected by the humidity. The food is also prepared to be eaten right away. China has a continental climate and is very dry, which means that there is less perspiration. Consequently, the custom of bathing has not developed as much. The four seasons are relatively dry and because of the wide range in daily temperature, they use beds.

In Korea, summers are extremely hot and winters are extremely cold. Therefore, houses were made of material that is less affected by temperature fluctuations. Furthermore, the *ondol*온돌 system which heats the floors has traditionally enticed Koreans to sit on the floor.

For the uninitiated, these three countries may seem alike. And while there are similarities, there are also big differences. For example, if you look at traditional attire, the Chinese costume is very tight fitting, bringing out the shape of the body. Also, since China historically did not have an *ondol* system, they had to wear lots of clothing to keep warm. Chinese food is fried or stir-fried about 70% of the time and only after you have eaten the main dishes do you eat rice. The spices used in Chinese food also differ greatly from those used in Korean cuisine. Moreover, even in the middle of the summer, the Chinese drink hot tea. The Chinese avoid cold drinks—even their beer and

[jwasik munhwa] 좌식문화

coke is lukewarm—because they think that it will cause stomachaches. The Chinese do not take off their shoes when they are at home because they do not sit or sleep on the floor, which is why they sometimes feel uncomfortable when they visit a Korean home.

If you visit Korean royal palaces or traditional homes, you will notice that the furniture doesn't have any legs. The *ondol* heating system is unique to Korea and has always ensured that Koreans could survive the long and cold winter months. In order to benefit from the *ondol* system, it was important to sit on the floor. Alternatively, in the hot summer months, it was cool and refreshing to sit on the floor.

If you go to a Korean restaurant, you will often be given a choice between sitting at a Western table or at a Korean table, which entails taking off your shoes. The advantage of the Korean sitting culture is that more people can be accommodated. Whether to sleep or sit, if everybody doesn't have a set place, it is easier to squeeze one more person in. This is also possible because unlike Western culture, which considers personal space to be very important, for Koreans such a concept is relatively less important. For this reason, Koreans tend to stand or sit closer to each other when speaking. As a result, it is not unusual to see Koreans take off their shoes and sit in the lotus position even on Western style chairs or to put one leg up on the chair as if they were sitting on the floor.

In today's modern homes, you will see Western style dining tables, beds, and sofas. However, even if there is a sofa, it is not considered improper, but rather more homey to sit on the floor to chat. For smaller homes, people will often do without such furniture since it takes up so much space.

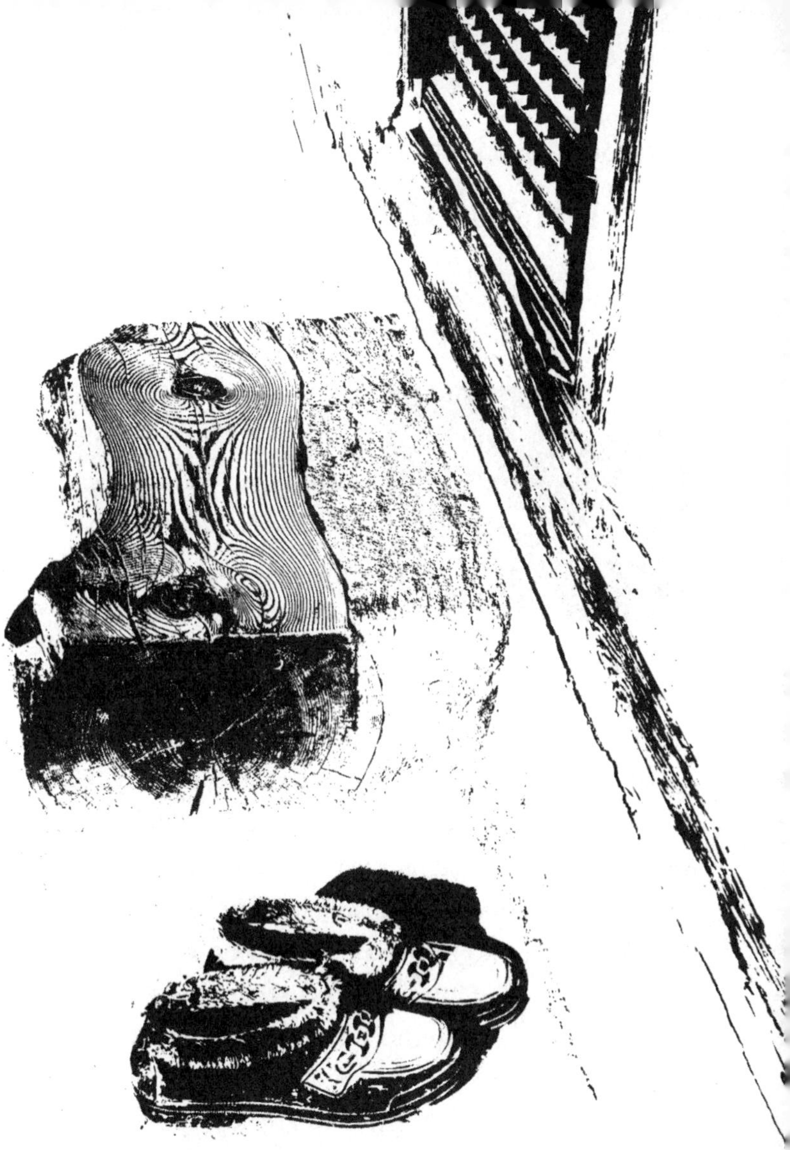

The Best of Both Worlds
Getting Married

Weddings in Korea can be divided into traditional Korean weddings and Western weddings, which can further be subdivided into Western-style or Christian weddings.

Let's look at traditional weddings first. When parents had a son or daughter of marrying age, they would contact a matchmaker. The *saju*사주 of both (the year, month, day, and time of birth) were exchanged, and if the fortune teller did not foresee any major calamity, the date would be set by the bride's family because they had to consider the bride's menstrual cycle. The bride and groom would see each other for the first time on their wedding night. Once the date was set, preparations got underway in both households. The first step after setting the date was for the groom's mother to send a *ham*함, or marriage chest, to the bride. In the past, couriers or house servants would carry the chest and "sell" it. Today, though this tradition is still carried on, it is usually the friends of the groom who carry it. Even today, the early evening calm may be broken by shouts of "*Ham saseyo!*함 사세요" (Buy a marriage chest!). Since the bride's family doesn't want to cause too much commotion in the neighborhood, the bride's family resorts to bribing the *ham* carriers to move closer to the house. This is quite a fun event. The "horse" who has to carry the heavy *ham*—preferably a married friend with a son—wears a mask of dried squid, and only budges if the "horseman" gives the command. In order to entice the group to move forward, the bride's

결혼 [gyeolhon]

friends come out and use their feminine wiles—singing songs, dancing and offering drinks.

Once the entourage enters the bride's home, everybody enjoys the feast set out by the bride's mother. Grooms in the old days traveled on horseback to the bride's house. Weddings were held in the bride's yard to ensure that everybody would be able to attend. This was the only day commoners were allowed to wear formal court costumes. Upon his arrival, the groom would present a wild goose to the bride's mother. Since wild geese mate for life, this gift was a symbol of the groom's promise that he would devote himself to his future bride. A live goose was used in the past, but today they have been replaced with wooden geese. It is easy to discern the female goose because she will have a string tied around her beak to ensure that she doesn't nag her husband. While the groom waited outside, the bride was carefully escorted by two assistants. The two faced each other for the first time during the ceremony and exchanged ceremonial bows. The bride bowed twice, and the groom reciprocated with one bow. This was done twice. Since this was the first meeting, the bride and groom would often sneak peeks to see what the other looked like. A gourd dipper was then used to serve wine to the bride and groom. The gourd, once whole, was then cut in half—symbolizing man and wife.

During a traditional wedding, you will also see a rooster wrapped in a blue cloth and a hen wrapped in a red one—the two wedding colors. Symbolically, the rooster's crow signals the beginning of a new day or a bright new beginning. The sound also chases away evil spirits. Another reason these animals are used is because they symbolize fecundity. Since the hen lays many eggs, the wish is for the bride to have many children. The last part of the wedding was the *pyebaek*폐백, something that is still conducted in today's modern weddings. The bride gives deep ceremonial bows to her in-laws and then the bride and groom sit together to pay their respects to the groom's family. The mother-in-law throws jujubes, or dates into the bride's veil and wishes them lots of sons—rather than daughters. Only the in-laws are allowed to attend this event. Nowadays, however, the more liberal families have a *pyebaek* for the bride's family as well.

What about modern weddings? It's a little bit of this, a little bit of that. They are often held in wedding halls or, for those with the means, in top hotels. When Westerners go to Korean weddings, they are often baffled by the fact that most of the guests seem to be totally unconcerned about what is actually going on, and more interested in talking amongst each other or eating. The simple reason for this is that often the wedding guests do not know the bride or groom; they are merely acquaintances of their parents or siblings. Therefore, they have to show up but will not be terribly interested in the wedding itself.

At a modern wedding, the master of ceremonies is usually a close friend of the groom, sort of like the best man. He will move things along during the wedding itself. When he gives the word, the groom will enter by himself. The bride will then enter accompanied by her father. The officiator will then give a brief speech—often describing the groom and bride, their background, and telling them how to live a happy married life. He—because it will invariably be a man—does not have to be a man of the cloth. He could be the head of the clan, a close friend of the father or a professor from university. After the speech, the bride and groom exchange vows and then bow to their parents, thanking them for their upbringing. Then they march down the aisle. Things start to become chaotic because it is time for the photo shoot, which is often considered the most important part of the event! First, it's a shot with the officiator, then the groom's parents, the bride's parents, both sets of parents, the groom's relatives, the bride's relatives, the groom's friends and then finally the bride's friends. After the photo session, the bride and groom will make the rounds of the guests who are enjoying themselves at the banquet.

What do you do as a guest? When you receive an invitation, you do not have to RSVP. You either go or you don't, and if you don't go you can apologize the next time you see the person. When you arrive at the wedding hall or hotel, sign the guestbook and hand in your envelope. If you have a gift, you can give it, but if possible, it is better to do so in advance, before the wedding. The couple will usually be leaving for their honeymoon right after the wedding and will be able to open it only after they return. Plus, in the chaos, it could get lost. If you are close to either the bride or groom, stay for the ceremony and be sure to take the all-important picture. They may not be able to remember whether or not you attended! Then you can go and enjoy the feast.

Food at a wedding

At today's weddings, you will be served either a Korean-style meal, often *galbitang* 갈비탕 or a Western-style meal, depending on where the wedding is held. Regardless of where it is held, there will always be noodles and *tteok* 떡 (rice cakes). The rice cakes, part of all Korean ceremonies, are indispensable. At weddings, noodles symbolize longevity and a happy life. They are so important that they have become ingrained in the Korean language. The expression "When are you going to treat me to noodles?" means "When are you getting married?"

Dating in Korea

In Konglish (a hybrid of Korean and English), a "meeting" is a casual group date, usually among college students. This started back in the 1970s when the dating scene became more liberal. Still, it was difficult to meet those of the other sex, and so these arranged group meetings were held. This is quite a vision to behold. On one side of the table, there might be 4-5 young women. On the other, there would be the same number of young men who would then choose their partner. Creative ways to choose a partner have been devised, but the most common way is to have the men submit an object that belongs to them — a pen or watch, for example — and then have the women choose one.

Since the meetings are large groups of students, the probability of meeting "the love of your life" is minimal. The meeting evolved into *sogaeting* 소개팅 — a compound word composed of *sogae* 소개, which means "to introduce" and the *ting* 팅 suffix from "meeting." This is a one-on-one arranged date by a middle person who preferably knows both people. Both group meetings and *sogaeting* are casual dates, meaning that the families are not involved. Of course, if things get serious, then the prearranged procedure would be followed.

Matchmaking

Considered archaic in the West, matchmaking has proven successful in many countries. The advantage is that the families can ensure that the bride or groom comes from a similar background and meets various conditions. Marrying simply for love can be catastrophic after love fizzles out. Today, there are matchmakers, little old ladies who have connections or matchmaking companies that have an entire database and find matches based on a computerized system, to carry this out. In either case, the two sides must connect before any decision is made about marriage.

Death, C'est la vie

Death is a fact of life that we all have to face at one time or another. The traditional funeral in Korea has evolved in line with modern times and schedules.

During the Joseon 조선 dynasty, a family would mourn the deceased for three years or at the very least a year and a half. Since that is impractical, today there are usually three (or less commonly) to five days' wakes. If you go to rural areas, you may have seen small, well-kept mounds strategically placed on the mountainside. These are burial grounds. If you visit Gyeongju 경주 you can visit kings' tombs that are the size of a small house. Because of overpopulation and some excesses with the tombstones, the government began to encourage people to opt for cremation.

When somebody passes away, the family will contact their friends, who will then often take it upon themselves to contact everybody else they know. In Korea, even if you do not know the deceased personally but only someone related to him/her, it is important that you pay your respects. As in the West, you should wear black, but white is also acceptable. The family will usually wear white. Avoiding red and yellow is a must, since they are colors related with happy events. For women, it used to be that you couldn't wear makeup, but it is now acceptable so as long as you avoid vivid red lipstick.

장례 [jangnye]

When to go: Unless you're very close—almost like family—and have to go to help out the family, it is better to wait until they are ready to greet the mourners. Since wakes usually last three days, a visit on the second day is your safest bet.

What to do: When you arrive at the funeral home—today they are usually located at big hospitals—sign the visitors' book and then offer an envelope. This is part of the wedding and funeral culture, and helps cover the expenses of the function. Depending on how close you are (or sometimes, on how much of an impression you want to make) the amount will vary. About $50 is considered average—neither offensive nor too impressive. After, you will enter the room in which the photograph of the deceased, along with ritual food and flowers (white chrysanthemums) will be displayed. If you like, you can offer some incense to the deceased. Then make two deep bows and one half-bow or simply bow your head and say a quick prayer, after which you bow to the principal male mourner and say a few words of regret.

After the formal portion of paying your respects, there will be some food prepared for the mourners. It is important to stay and eat the food prepared. Don't be surprised to see people laughing and enjoying themselves. The saddest wake is when there is nobody present or there are only a few mourners. Koreans take this as an opportunity to meet up with friends and acquaintances they haven't seen in a long time. Naturally, it shouldn't be taken to extremes, but it is polite to stay at least an hour.

The shroud

The lunar year is about 11 days shorter than the solar calendar. Therefore, every three years one month — and every eight years three months — must be added to the lunar calendar in order to make the proper adjustment, just like in the solar calendar every fourth year is a leap year. If this adjustment were not made, in a span of 17 years it would snow in May or June.

The leap month was considered a "rotten month" and therefore it was a time when the heavens and gods loosened their supervision of humans and so even if something disrespectful occurred during this period, one could avoid the gods' wrath. It is for this reason that during leap month, burial sites were changed and shrouds were bought. Even today, if children buy a shroud for their parents during this time, it is said that the parents will live a long life. The shroud had to be completed in one day, and was stored in tobacco or mint leaves, which repelled moths. In the past, they were made of silk but today hempcloth is used more often.

Since the shroud is used to dress the dead, it has great symbolic significance and also gives insight into how Koreans view death. First, it is part of a rite of passage, much like wedding garb. Therefore, on the day that the shroud is made, neighbors and friends get together and make a feast of this event. Afterwards, the shroud is said to be a source of comfort and the owner takes it out of the closet from time to time to admire it. Second, there are several taboos linked to the manufacture of the shroud. In addition, it has to be made in a leap month and must be completed in one day, a single thread must be used, and the ends cannot be tied together.

As such, the shroud has traditionally been seen in a positive light as the last ceremonial garb a person wears. Even though it is a sad event, Koreans do not view in a negative way: Earthly life is over, but it is followed by a new beginning in the afterlife.

Traditionally, funerals lasted five days, nine for the well-to-do and 25 for the nobility. Thus, there was ample time to prepare the shroud. However, today in most cases it lasts for only three days, which doesn't allow enough time. It is also considered an act of piety to prepare the shroud for one's parents because it is a source of comfort for them. It is customary to prepare the shroud after the 60th birthday.

Not in red!

In the West, it is not unusual to write a person's name with a red pen. In fact, nobody thinks twice about it. However, in Korea, this is discomforting and even shocking. If you do so in front of a Korean, he/she will either give you another pen or tell you not to do so.

The only time that you write somebody's name in red is when they have passed away. On top of the coffin, a banner with the person's lineage and the person's name is written in red.

Thanks to my ancestors

In Korea, ancestors are revered as almost god-like. This is an expression of filial piety. Even to this day, when one's parents pass away, people will go out of their way to provide the best burial grounds — even if it is beyond their means. By giving their ancestors the best treatment, even in their afterlife, people believe that they, in turn, will be looked after. Even now, if something good happens to them, they will unhesitatingly say, "It's thanks to my ancestors." For precisely this reason, cremation has met with great resistance. However, over the years, people have come to realize that burials are no longer a viable solution in a country with such limited land space.

The Korean Way
Counting Your Age

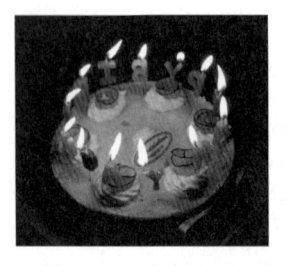

The question of Korean age and Western age often confuses visitors from abroad. For a brief explanation, read on:

Date: August 12, 2006

Q: I was born on December 12, 1991 and I'm American. I still haven't turned 16, that is I'm 15 years and 9 months old. I have to wait three months before I can legally drive. But I have a Korean friend who goes to my school, and she was born in November 1991, but she insists that she's 16. Does that mean that she can drive? Do Koreans count their age differently than Americans?

A: To give you the quick answer, the answer is no and yes. The answer to the first question is that since you're living in the States, age must be counted the American way, and therefore your Korean friend cannot drive. For the second question, while in the US, you start counting from the time you are born. In Korea, babies are already a year old when they are born because the time that they were in their mother's womb is also counted. I hope I've answered your question.

When asked one's age in Korea, it is not unusual to answer twice—one might say, "My Korean age is 30, but my *man*만 age is 28." If you've already celebrated your birthday, you add one year to your birthday, if not, you add two years. The reason is as mentioned above, because you need to count the nine months you were in your mother's womb. In the West, when you are born you are not a year old. However, in Korea, you are already a year old. That is why a newborn child's 100th day is so important in Korea. It technically completes the full year.

나이 | [nai]

Why do you want to know my age?

When meeting a foreigner for the first time, Koreans automatically inquire about age and marital status, and raise other personal questions which usually lead to embarrassment or irritation — or both — for the foreigner. The reason for these personal questions is that in order to use the proper level of Korean language, a speaker must be clued in on their counterpart's social standing in relation to their own. Once this is known, they will be able to select the appropriate language for the conversation. Personal questions, therefore, are simply the necessary first step toward structuring the dialog appropriately.

While Western culture is generally based on horizontal relationships, those of Korea adhere to a strict vertical system in which position, age and education are key elements. Among alumni, even the year of graduation is a determining variable. It is according to these variables that the hierarchy is established, which, in turn, automatically influences the language.

Birthday feast

On your birthday, you will invariably have *miyeokguk*미역국, or seaweed soup. It is full of iron and extremely healthful. Though Koreans love it, foreigners tend to think that it's slimy! After giving birth, women will eat *miyeokguk* soup for breakfast, lunch and dinner for at least one month. Since childbirth entails a loss of blood, the seaweed, which is filled with iron, is very helpful in replenishing the blood.

However, a mother would never give her child *miyeokguk* before an important test. The slippery quality of miyeokguk has a negative connotation — during the test, the answers could slip one's mind.

Counting Moons
The Lunar Calendar

Before January 1, 1896, when Korea started using the Gregorian calendar, Koreans used the lunar calendar, which is divided into 24 seasonal points, each lasting about 15 days. The lunar calendar was important because it marked important days for the farmers. Though it is not as prominent today, traditional festivals are celebrated according to the lunar calendar, and older Koreans may celebrate their birthdays according to the lunar calendar.

Seollal 설날 Lunar New Year's Day
- *EVENTS* An ancestral service is offered before the grave of one's ancestors, New Year's greetings are exchanged with family, relatives and neighbors. The ritual of bowing, *sebae* 세배, to elders is performed.
- *LUNAR CALENDAR DATE* Day 1 of month 1
- *FOOD* Sliced rice cakes in soup, fried honey cakes

Daeboreum 대보름 First Full Moon
- *EVENTS* Talisman burning to ward off evil spirits
- *LUNAR CALENDAR DATE* Day 15 of month 1
- *FOOD* Rice boiled with five grains, nuts (walnuts, peanuts, etc.) and wine

Junghwajeol 중화절 Start of Farming Season
- *EVENTS* Housecleaning, coming of age ceremony, fishermen's shaman rite
- *LUNAR CALENDAR DATE* Day 1 of month 2
- *FOOD* Stuffed, pine-flavored rice cakes

음력 [eumnyeok]

Samjinnal 삼짇날 Migration of Swallows Return
- *EVENTS* Wrestling, fortune telling
- *LUNAR CALENDER DATE* Day 3 of month 3
- *FOOD* Azalea pancake

Hansik 한식 Visiting of Ancestral Graves
- *EVENTS* Visit ancestral grave
- *LUNAR CALENDER DATE* 105 days after winter solstice
- *FOOD* Cold food only: mugwort cake, mugwort dumplings, mugwort soup

Dano 단오 Spring Festival
- *EVENTS* Swinging, wrestling
- *LUNAR CALENDER DATE* Day 5 of month 5
- *FOOD* Rice cake with herbs, herring soup

Yudu 유두 Greeting of Water
- *EVENTS* Water greeting, washing hair to wash away bad luck
- *LUNAR CALENDER DATE* Day 15 of month 6
- *FOOD* Five-colored noodles, rice dumplings

Chilseok 칠석 The Seventh Day of the Seventh Month
- *EVENTS* Rite praying for rain
- *LUNAR CALENDER DATE* Day 7 of month 7
- *FOOD* Wheat pancakes, rice cakes with red beans

Baekjung 백중 Worship of Buddha
- *EVENTS* Worship Buddha
- *LUNAR CALENDER DATE* Day 15 of month 7
- *FOOD* Mixed rice cake

Chuseok 추석 Harvest Festival
- *EVENTS* Visit ancestral grave, offering of earliest rice grain
- *LUNAR CALENDER DATE* Day 15 of month 8
- *FOOD* Pine-flavored rice cakes stuffed with chestnuts, sesame or beans, taro soup

Jungyangjeol 중양절 Celebrating Autumn
- *EVENTS* Celebrating autumn with poetry and painting, composing poetry, enjoying nature
- *LUNAR CALENDER DATE* Day 9 of month 9
- *FOOD* Chrysantheum pancakes, roe, honey citron tea

Dongji 동지 Winter Solstice
- *EVENTS* Rites to dispel bad spirits
- *LUNAR CALENDER DATE* December 22 according to the solar calendar
- *FOOD* Red bean soup with rice dumplings

Seotdal geumeum 섣달그믐 New Year's Eve
- *EVENTS* Staying up all night long with all doors open to receive ancestral spirits
- *LUNAR CALENDER DATE* Day 31 of month 12
- *FOOD* Mixed rice with vegetables, bean powder rice cakes, traditional biscuits

The Korean Zodiac

"What's your sign?" is the oldest pick-up line ever in the West. But it would never be used in Asia because the "sign" immediately indicates the person's age. The Oriental zodiac is not based on months but rather on years. Each year is designated the year of an animal and everybody born in that year has the same zodiac sign. For a more accurate reading, it is important to have not only the exact year, but also the month, day and time of birth.

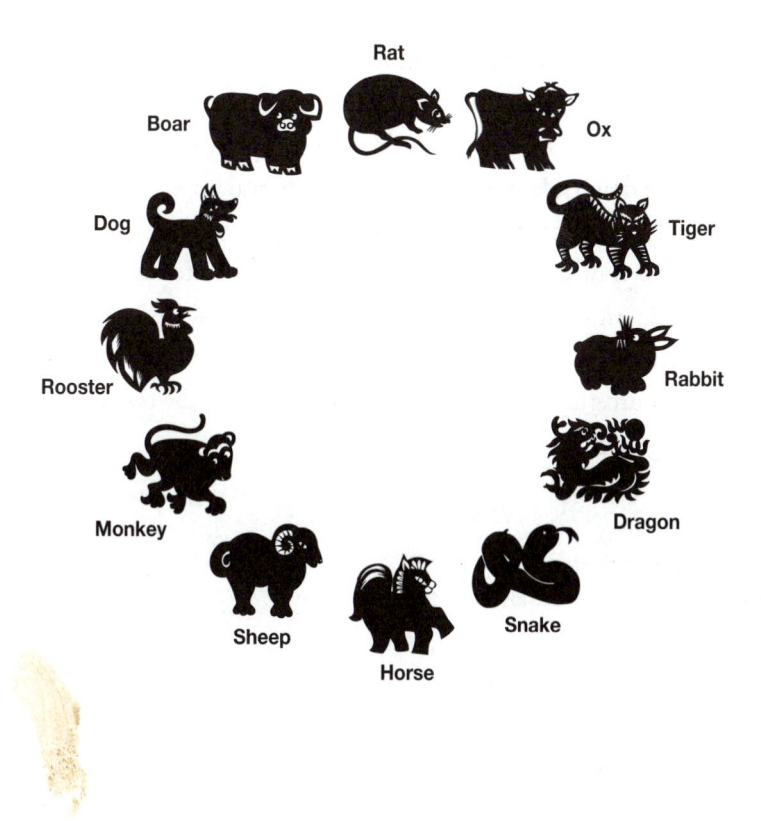

The Year of the Rat
1912, 1924, 1936, 1948, 1960, 1972, 1984, 1996, 2008, 2020

On the first day of the year, the heavenly god said that whichever animal was the first to arrive at heaven's gate would be given the first place in the Oriental zodiac. The cow diligently set off early and was the first to arrive. However, the rat had hitched a free ride on the cow's back, and as soon as they got to the gate, the rat jumped off the cow's back and was the first to arrive. Therefore, the Oriental zodiac begins with the rat.

People born in the year of the Rat are very honest, almost too honest. Sometimes your honesty hurts your friendships, and because of this, you seldom make lasting friendships. You are very ambitious and want nothing more than to succeed in life. You have a lively imagination and are smart. On the downside, you tend to be greedy and opportunistic, as well as a busybody. In the area of money, however, you lack the self-discipline to keep any in your bank account. You are best suited to be an artist, real estate agent or critic. You are most compatible with dragons, who will give you strength, oxen, who will give you stability, or monkeys, who give you their resourcefulness. Definitely avoid the horse; the two of you will always be arguing.

● *KOREAN EXPRESSION*
쥐도 새도 모르게 *jwido saedo moreuge*
Without a mouse or bird knowing.
Without anybody knowing.

The Year of the Ox
1913, 1925, 1937, 1949, 1961, 1973, 1985, 1997, 2009, 2021

Bright, patient and inspiring to others. You work best by yourself and tend to be very introverted. Because of your patience, you make a great parent. You are a hard worker and responsible. You don't get angry easily and are logical and balanced. Your only fault is that you sometimes let friendships slip because of your shyness. You can also be stubborn, arrogant and authoritative. There is no romance. When you do get angry, you tend to explode with fury and you can't control yourself. Allow yourself to open up and you will find a world full of treasures in friendships. You are best suited to be a farmer, architect, chef, surgeon or police officer. The best mate for you is either a snake, who has the wisdom to humor you all the time, a mouse, who will be faithful to you forever, or a rooster, who is on the same conservative wavelength. Stay away from the sheeps and tigers.

● *KOREAN EXPRESSION*

지나가는 소가 웃을 일 *jinaganeun soga useul il*
Something that a passing cow would laugh at.

The cow is an animal that does not react sensitively to things that happen around it. Because it is a relatively big animal, it has few enemies and therefore does not fear other animals. It not only is indifferent to what happens around it, but it is also oblivious to even the most overt action. If such a cow were to laugh, you can imagine how funny it must be. However, it can also be used negatively to mean that something is so ridiculous that even a cow would laugh at it.

The Year of the Tiger
1914, 1926, 1938, 1950, 1962, 1974, 1986, 1998, 2010, 2022

Ferocious is the only way to describe the feisty tiger. Some of your best personality traits are honor, tolerance and courage. You are consistent and strong, a leader. But for every good trait, there is also a bad trait. Sometimes you can be very stubborn, a bit of a rebel and almost too aggressive that it sometimes turns people off. You also tend to pick fights. You are best suited to be a foreman, stuntman, state leader or a bullfighter. Your best mate is a horse, for its sincerity, or a boar because it suffers difficult situations. A dog also makes a good mate for you. A monkey will act loyal but in the end make a fool of you.

● *KOREAN EXPRESSION*

호랑이가 물어가도 정신만 차리면 산다. *horang-iga mureogado jeongsinman charimyeon sanda*
Even if a tiger drags you away, if you keep your wits about you, you will survive.
In a difficult situation, as long as you remain cool and level-headed, you will be able to find a solution.

The Year of the Rabbit
1915, 1927, 1939, 1951, 1963, 1975, 1987, 1999, 2011, 2023

The luckiest of all signs, a person with this sign is very talented and articulate. Affectionate, yet sometimes shy, you seek harmony throughout your life. You are very adaptable, graceful and intelligent, and have a discerning eye. You are also very sophisticated and sociable. At the same time you are sincere and thorough. The downside is that you tend to be emotional and hesitant. You get angry easily and can be superficial. Sometimes you are unpredictable and selfish. Your best bet is to become a model, interior designer, collector, critic, journalist, lawyer or actor. You are most compatible with sheep because you share the same hobbies; dogs, because they are sincere; and boars, because they are thorough. Stay away from roosters because you will not be able to put up with their vanity. Also, the rabbit can always sense a tiger's deception and will not tolerate any interference from it.

● *KOREAN EXPRESSION*
두 마리 토끼 잡으려다 두 마리 다 놓친다. *du mari tokki jabeuryeoda du mari da nochinda*
Try to catch two rabbits at once and miss both.
You can't catch two birds with one stone.

The Year of the Dragon
1916, 1928, 1940, 1952, 1964, 1976, 1988, 2000, 2012, 2024

The dragon sign is one of the most complex and mysterious of all signs in the zodiac. You love life and are lucky to have abundant health to enjoy all the things that you want to do. The dragon is strong and full of energy, which makes it attractive. You are direct and successful. You are extroverted and filled with convictions. You are always on the go, and you always have a lot of demands. You tend to be reckless and a little threatening. You are overconfident and arrogant. You are always in a rush and not terribly witty. You veer off course easily—very talkative. Your best bet is to become an artist, architect, manufacturer, lawyer, doctor, shop owner or missionary. You are most compatible with a rat because of its warm heart or a snake because you have the same sense of humor. A rooster—which is boastful—will contribute to your success, and a monkey will complement your strength. Avoid any dogs like the plague!

● KOREAN EXPRESSION
용꿈 *yongkkum*
A dragon dream.
Before the birth of a child, it is not unusual to have a conception dream. This can be dreamt by the parents, a relative or even friends. Among the many dreams possible, a dragon is considered to be the best. One where a dragon is in the sky is considered to augur well for the child. This means that the child will hold a high government position or enjoy talent and world acclaim.

The Year of the Snake
1917, 1929, 1941, 1953, 1965, 1977, 1989, 2001, 2013, 2025

The snake is very wise and popular. Instinctive and calm, at the same time it has strong charisma. You are tender and elegant. You are also your worst critic. You are possessive, which means that you have a jealous streak. You can be cold and lazy, as well as stingy. You are most likely to have an affair. There is a tendency to be very vain and attracted to physical beauty. Another of your negative characteristics is your temper, which sometimes gets you into trouble. You need to learn how to relax and not always blow your top. Despite your flaws, you are a very intense person with a lot of wisdom, which you are happy to share with others. You are best suited to be a teacher, writer, psychiatrist, diplomat, real estate agent or politician. You are most compatible with an ox, who can make you happy, a rooster, with whom you will fight but at the same time complement each other, or a dragon, who will share its wisdom with you. Avoid tigers and boars.

● *KOREAN EXPRESSION*
용두사미 *yongdu sami*
A dragon's head with a snake's tail.
This is an expression that is often used to mean an anticlimax. A similar expression in English is "to start with a bang and end with a whimper."

The Year of the Horse

1918, 1930, 1942, 1954, 1966, 1978, 1990, 2002, 2014, 2026

The horse is very popular and always at the center of attention—at least it tries to be. If you're a horse, watch out for the opposite sex—they are drawn to you because of your charm and popularity. Sometimes, though, because the horse is always at the center of attention, you can be ostentatious and impatient if you don't get your own way. Although you are not a needy person, you like to draw attention to yourself and be noticed by others. You're witty and sociable. You are also realistic, independent and very convincing. Since you are usually at the center of attention, you tend to be self-centered and overly energetic. You are inconsiderate of others and quick to get angry. You have contradictory personality traits. You're like a child, not very careful and unpredictable. You change your mind often and lack willpower. You are also afraid of failing. Your best bet is to become a pharmacist, physicist, doctor, politician, adventure-seeker, writer, pilot or bartender. You are most compatible with a tiger, who is on your same wavelength, or a dog, who will let you do your own thing. Your worst match is the rat. Also, one horse year every 60 years is called the year of the white horse. The last one was in 1990 and the next will be in 2050. It is said that those who are born in the year of the white horse are extremely strong-willed and their lives will not be trouble-free. The myth can actually be traced back to Japan. A long time ago, a Japanese landlord had a daughter who was born in the year of the white horse. She faced a lot of hardships and did not have an easy life. She also made life miserable for the people around her. Even today, people tend to avoid having children in the year of the white horse, especially daughters.

● *KOREAN EXPRESSION*

새옹지마 ***sae-ong jima***

Saeong's horse.

This saying is equivalent of "every cloud has a silver living." This phrase comes from a story about the horse of an old man named Sae-ong 새옹. A long time ago, an old man had the misfortune of losing his horse. Later the horse that had run away returned with an excellent steed. Unfortunately, the old man's son broke his leg while riding the new horse. Yet this turned out for the best because a war had just broken out and the son managed to avoid the draft thanks to his broken leg. What this story goes to show is that in life, misfortunes follow fortune and vice versa, and therefore we should not be overly emotional but take things in stride.

The Year of the Sheep

1919, 1931, 1943, 1955, 1967, 1979, 1991, 2003, 2015, 2027

Sheep are very quiet people who place high value on their personal life and keeping it that way—personal. If you are a sheep, you thrive for excellence, and are always looking for a challenge so you can demonstrate your creative side. The sheep is very polite and understanding, as well as peaceful and truthful. You are very lucky and adaptable. There is also a romantic side to you. Although sheep display a greater elegance than any of the other signs, they can also be very timid and constantly need reassuring and an occasional ego massage. You tend to be irresponsible and have a weak will. There is a pessimistic streak in you and you are always hesitant. You are sensitive and do not manage your money too well. You should become a technician, actor, artist, gardener or professional dancer. You are most compatible with the rabbit. You also get along wonderfully with the boar, who will control financial matters, and the horse, who will ensure that your love lasts. Avoid the ox at all costs!

● *KOREAN EXPRESSION*

양처럼 순하다. *yangcheoreom sunhada*

As meek as a sheep.

In English, lambs are also described as meek.

The Year of the Monkey
1920, 1932, 1944, 1956, 1968, 1980, 1992, 2004, 2016, 2028

Monkeys are very intelligent and able to influence people. But sometimes you think you're better than you really are. This leads others to think you are cocky and full of yourself. An enthusiastic achiever, the monkey tries to excel in everything. Monkeys make great lovers because you're always trying to please your partners (monkeys want to master everything—even in the bedroom). The monkey is very talented and observant. The monkey's flaw is its confusion and inability to resolve personal turmoil. Some of its actions are looked at askance by others. The monkey is best suited to be a business person, writer, advertisement director or diplomat. Monkeys are compatible with dragons, who give them strength, and rats, who make them happy. But they should stay away from tigers—sparks will fly!

● *KOREAN EXPRESSION*

원숭이도 나무에서 떨어진다. *wonsung-ido namueseo tteoreojinda*

Even a monkey can fall from a tree.

The English equivalent would be "Even Homer sometimes nods," meaning that even if it's something that you're used to doing, you can sometimes make mistakes.

The Year of the Rooster
1921, 1933, 1945, 1957, 1969, 1981, 1993, 2005, 2017, 2029

Roosters are workaholics, devoted to work and the quest for knowledge. Roosters are naturally ambitious and want the best from life. You realize that if you work hard now, you can play later. Roosters are honorable and filled with conviction. You have an active imagination but do not tell lies. You have a strong sense of adventure. You can create something from nothing. However, because you are so determined to succeed roosters often neglect friendships and loved ones. You can sometimes be selfish, only looking out for your own interests. You are a dreamer and like to boast. You can be aggressive when expressing yourself.

You are best suited to be an advertiser, traveler, beauty expert, doctor or soldier. You are very compatible with the ox. Roosters and dragons make the perfect couple because you share the same ideals. You are also compatible with the snake—you will spend your lives praising each other. Rabbits are trouble for the rooster.

● *KOREAN EXPRESSION*
암탉이 울면 집안이 망한다. *amtagi ulmyeon jibani manghanda*
If the hen cries, it will bring a house down.
It used to be that women were supposed to keep their mouths shut, so when a woman was outspoken, men would use this expression. Many Koreans believe that this is a Korean expression, but it is actually mentioned more often in China and Japan.

The Year of the Dog
1922, 1934, 1946, 1958, 1970, 1982, 1994, 2006, 2018, 2030

Dogs make great team leaders because they work so well with others. You are very loyal and honest. Whenever there is a problem, the person everyone turns to is the dog. The dog is devoted and trustworthy. You are very responsible and are always very careful. Hardworking, you are always willing to help out. Dogs are very generous but sometimes only when it suits you. Occasionally you can be very selfish and stubborn. You can be direct and defensive, even anti-social and combative at times. You are wary of others. You are best suited to be a construction supervisor, critic, missionary, judge, private investigator, politician, manager or scholar. You are most compatible with the horse. Tigers make a good marriage partner. You also work well with rabbits, but the relationship hinges on the efforts made by the dog. The worst partner for a dog is the dragon because of the dog's devotion and idealism.

● KOREAN EXPRESSION
서당 개 삼년이면 풍월을 읊는다. *seodang gae samnyeonimyeon pung-woreul eumneunda*
Even the village school dog can write poetry after three years.
An approximate expression in English would be "the sparrow near a school sings the primer."

The Year of the Boar
1923, 1935, 1947, 1959, 1971, 1983, 1995, 2007, 2019, 2031

As a boar, you are a very chivalrous and noble animal. You keep lifelong friendships due to your kindness and friendly personality. You are fair and truthful. On the other hand, you tend to be impulsive. You love peace and are confident and generous. You are popular, outgoing and sociable. However, you are easily deceived because you can be too naive. You're stubborn and become sad easily. You cannot stand up to temptation and find it difficult to say no. You are best suited to work in the film industry or to be a doctor, architect, manufacturer, writer, painter, entertainer or scientist. You are most compatible with the rabbit, sheep and snake. You are able to avoid quarrels with rabbits. Sheeps understand your caprices, and tigers determine the outcome of your relationship. Avoid the snake, which will wrap itself around you so that you can't move.

● KOREAN EXPRESSION
돼지처럼 먹는다. *dwaejicheoreom meongneunda*
To eat like a pig.
In English, to eat like a pig means to eat in a sloppy manner, but in Korean it means to eat a lot.

Counseling Korean Style
The Fortune Telling

Fortune telling is deeply ingrained in the Korean way of life. Basically, it can be divided into two types: on the one hand, there is the more scientific fortune telling, which entails a reading of the time, day, month and year of birth, and on the other, there is the more shamanistic type, in which the reader is possessed by spirits. There is also palm, face and foot reading, but these often accompany the other two types of readings.

When a child is born, the mother will often go to see a fortune teller to read the child's future because she wants to hear good things about her child. Then, throughout the child's life, at the beginning of each new year, when taking an important test such as the college entrance exam, deciding which college to apply to and at other turning points, the mother will again go to see a fortune teller. Before getting married, the mother will often seek a fortune teller's advice on whether or not the couple is compatible. If the fortune teller says that it is a doomed relationship or something equally serious, the parents will often reconsider. Sometimes, when the parents of either the young man or lady do not approve, but do not want to be too direct, they will use this as a face-saving excuse.

The fortune teller is actually like a counselor. Since visiting a psychiatrist is not widespread in Korea, having somebody to talk to, listen to problems and give advice is a way to relieve stress.

점 [jeom]

A day without *son*
In folklore, the *son*손 (wandering evil spirits) travel in the four cardinal directions — north, south, east and west — trying to interfere with human activity and generally being a nuisance. Therefore a day with *son* is a day when there will be a loss or damage because the evil spirits are on the move. It is for this reason that when one wants to choose an auspicious day — to move, for example — it is safer to choose a day without *son*. Even today, on such days, the movers will ask for a little bit more money, it is a day when business is excellent!

These spirits rise to the skies on the 9th, 10th, 19th, 20th, 29th and 30th days of each lunar month. Thus, these days are without *son*.

Colors, Striking a Balance

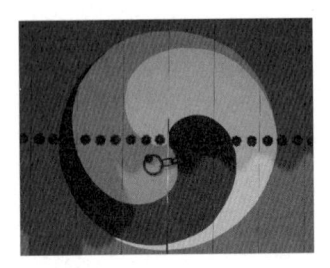

Korea's ancestors placed great importance on harmony and tried to find harmony within colors as well. Colors not only have esthetic relevance, but also cultural and religious significance, too.

Five colors are basic to Korea's indigenous religion: yellow symbolizes the center of the universe, it is the color of soil, and signifies the ever changing seasons and the importance of the earth; blue/green is creation, and as the color of the forest, relates to spring and the east; white is truth and expresses autumn and the west; red is creation and passion and corresponds with summer and the south; and black is human wisdom and water, as well as winter and the north.

These colors are used liberally in traditional Korean clothing as well as on roof eaves. As the central color, yellow was considered to be the noblest one, and therefore could only be worn by the king. Green represented creation and birth and therefore was used to chase away evil spirits. One of the reasons Koreans traditionally preferred to wear white was because white represents innocence, truth, life and purity. Red is equated with fire, blood and passion and was considered the most vibrant color. Black symbolizes water. These colors are also very present in traditional Korean weddings. The red circles that are placed on the bride's cheeks and forehead are supposed to chase away evil spirits. The red and green Korean *hanbok*한복 worn by a newly married bride symbolize longevity and wealth. The five-colored clothing that children wear on

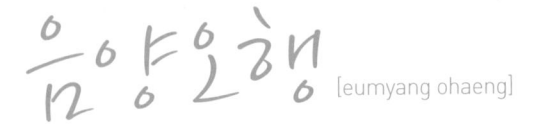

음양오행 [eumyang ohaeng]

their fifth birthday, and worn on other occasions as well, is meant to chase away evil spirits and ensure a long and healthy life.

These colors are also present in Korean food. In large earthen pots containing soy sauce, a string of red peppers is wrapped around the mouth to chase away bad spirits. Red bean congee and red bean rice cakes are meant to do the same. If you look carefully at the noodles served at festive occasions to ensure longevity, you will see five-colored toppings.

Koreans also used red earth for building their homes. When the New Year came around, a red charm was attached to the front gate to ward off evil spirits. On wooden buildings, especially the eaves, the *dancheong*단청, which consisted of the five basic colors, was painted. This served to preserve the building but was also decorative and added dignity to palaces and temples. Clearly, the five directional colors were not just colors, but symbolized directions and seasons, as well as religious meaning, since they were used to ward off evil spirits and wish for blessings.

Symbolism of the five colors

COLOR	DIRECTION	ELEMENT	SYMBOL
blue	east	wood	blue dragon
white	west	metal	white tiger
red	south	fire	red phoenix
black	north	water	black turtle
yellow	middle	earth	yellow dragon

Yin and *yang* philosophy

The philosophy of *yin* and *yang* has greatly influenced Korean thinking, traditions, society and history. *Yang* stands for the positive, active and expansive forces in the world, while *yin* stands for the passive and contractive forces. While the sky is *yang*, the earth is *yin*; the male is *yang* and the female *yin*. *Yin* and *yang* philosophy can be traced back to the Dangun단군 legend (And then Korea was created. See Part 1). The gods Hwanung환웅 and Hwanin환인 represent *yang*, while the bear and tiger on earth represent *yin*. Thus, Korea's founding father, Dangun, was born of the bear transformed into a woman, *yin*, with Hwanung representing *yang*. According to Eastern philosophy, everything can be described as both *yin* and *yang*. *Yin* and *yang* are opposites but no one thing is completely *yin* or completely *yang*. *Yin* and *yang* are interdependent, and cannot exist without the other. For example, the night is dark and therefore can be considered *yin*, but then dawn breaks and the sun rises and so the day becomes *yang*. Part of *yin* is in *yang* and part of *yang* is in *yin*. There are no absolutes in the world, because as soon as there is an absolute, it spills over to become the other.

Using Seals
Instead of Signatures

Sometimes called "chops," seals were used to prove one's identity on all different kinds of documents—much like the personal signature in the West.

There are many different kinds of seals that are used for different purposes, but the most important one is the *ingam*인감 seal, which is registered at a government office. Though it can be used much like a regular seal, the *ingam* seal is needed for important contracts. Traditionally, seals were made of stone, metal, wood or jade (among other materials) and were truly works of art.

In a recent Korean movie, *The Korean Peninsula*한반도, the national seal is at the center of the drama because it bestows legitimacy and sovereignty. Made of jade or gold, the royal seal was a symbol of authority and legitimacy, which was used in diplomatic and domestic documents and passed on to successive kings. In 1948, when the government of the Republic of Korea was established, the royal seal was replaced with the national seal.

Today, although they are used less often, seals are nevertheless still used for legal contracts—buying a home or car, for example, and at the bank, too.

[dojang] 도장

Lucky Numbers
Unlucky Numbers

Koreans do not like the number four because it is pronounced the same way as the Chinese character for death. Therefore it is not unusual to ride an elevator that has no fourth floor, or which instead of a "4" button has an "F" button. Also, table settings do not come in sets of four, but rather two, three, five or six. To accommodate Western sensibilities, there are some buildings that also skip the thirteenth floor, so a building that appears to have 16 floors actually has only 14—the fourth and thirteenth floor having been skipped.

Influenced by Western thinking, many Koreans today consider seven to be a lucky number. But traditionally, three was thought to be lucky. This is ingrained in the language as well. For example, when shouting *manse* 만세! (ten thousand lives), it is usually done three times. When playing games, the winner is often decided with three games (*samsepan* 삼세판 and *samsebeon* 삼세번). In *yin* and *yang* philosophy, three is thought to be the most harmonious combination because it signifies completion.

Rather than even numbers, Koreans tend to prefer odd numbers and for this reason when providing cash gifts at weddings or paying condolences at a funeral, either thirty or fifty thousand won is offered. Strictly speaking, these are even numbers but the number of bills is odd. Even tea sets or plates are sold in odd numbers.

숫자 [sutja]

Landmark birthdays

For Americans, the big 4-0 and 5-0 are considered turning points in a person's life, and are supposed to have a psychological impact. In Korea, people try to be careful when they are 29, 39, 49, 59 (the final years of a decade). The ninth year is seen as an obstacle that must be overcome.

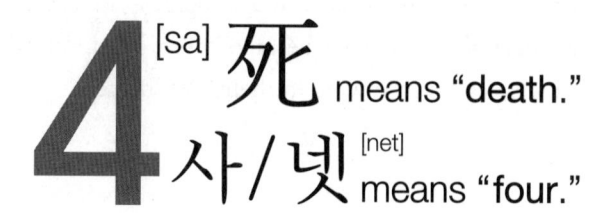

4 [sa] 死 means "death."
사 / 넷 [net] means "four."

Bringing the Right Gift

Koreans like to give gifts because it is an expression of their gratitude. If you give a gift to a Korean, don't be disappointed if they say thank you and then set it aside and almost ignore it. Traditionally, it is only after the person has left that the gift will be opened. However, since Koreans have become more Westernized, younger people will open gifts on the spot and at other times the gift giver might tell the person to open it right away. Food is the gift most often offered even today, although the items have changed somewhat. After the Korean War, when goods were scarce, a favorite gift was a carton of eggs; during the 1970s, before import liberalization, a bunch of bananas was considered a delicacy. (Korea is not a tropical country and therefore tropical fruits are all imported.) Even today, top quality fruit, meat and dried corvine (fish) are offered as gifts. For Seollal 설날 (Lunar New Year's Day) and Chuseok 추석 (Korean Thanksgiving), gifts of rice cakes, rice wine, fruit and meat are also exchanged among family members, but especially to those whom you would like to express your gratitude. On Parents' Day (May 8th) and Teacher's Day (May 15th), children and students give red carnations as an expression of their gratitude. In the past, guests at a housewarming party would bring matches, soap, cooking oil, or tissue paper to symbolize their wishes for great wealth and happiness in the new home. Nowadays, because Koreans have become more Westernized, they tend to bring flowers or a bottle wine to their host/hostess.

선물 [seonmul]

Spoons and Chopsticks

Koreans use a spoon and chopsticks when eating. All food is cut in the kitchen before being served, or will be cut at the table so that it is easy to grab with the chopsticks. If the food has not been cut, the chopsticks will be used to tear the food apart. If one person is having trouble, it is not unusual for another person to help out by using a chopstick as an anchor while the other person pulls the food apart. Korean spoons are not like Chinese-style spoons, but like Western soup spoons. It is considered improper to hold the chopsticks and spoon together at the same time. (Actually Westerners are amazed that Koreans are able to do so at all!) Since Korean rice is sticky, it is not difficult to pick it up with chopsticks. This is why it is considered improper to bring the rice bowl to your mouth. In fact, the rice and soup bowls should never leave the table. If you need to use a spoon to eat the rice because you have placed other food on top of it, be sure that you don't leave anything on your spoon. Also, never leave your spoon stuck in the rice. That is considered improper because it is done only during ancestral rites; that is, for dead ancestors.

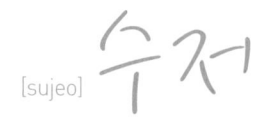

[sujeo] 수저

Korean Tales

Koreans will proudly tell you that their history dates back 5,000 years. Needless to say, Korean folklore is plentiful and colorful. Here are just a few examples.

Sim Cheong, the blind man's daughter

A long time ago, a poor blind *yangban* 양반 called Sim Hak-gyu 심학규 lived with his beloved wife. After many childless years, the wife gave birth to a beautiful baby girl whom they called Sim Cheong 심청. Sadly the mother died in childbirth. Sim Cheong was a devoted daughter who accompanied her father when he went begging for alms. One day, old man Sim 심 stumbled into a deep ditch. Fearing for his life, he yelled and yelled until he heard a voice. It said, "Old man, if you give 300 bushels of rice to Buddha at my temple, we will pray for the return of your sight." Old man Sim agreed and before he knew it, he was out of the ditch. It was only afterwards that he realized that he did not have the means to offer 300 bushels of rice to the temple. He recounted what had happened to him to his daughter. Worried about how to keep her father's promise, Sim Cheong fell into a fitful sleep. In her dreams her mother appeared. "Go to the harbor. There you will see a merchant looking for a young maiden. If you go with him, he will give you 300 bushels of rice."

The next day she went to the harbor. As it turned out, she was just what the merchants were looking for—a sacrifice to appease the Dragon King of the East Sea, who had been sinking ships on their way to China. They paid the 300 bushels of rice, and old man Sim took them to the temple, where the monks prayed for the return of his sight. But he did not regain his sight.

전래동화 [jeollae donghwa]

Meanwhile, on the ship, the waters soon turned choppy and ominous. The captain of the ship brought Sim Cheong, who was dressed as a bride, up to the plank. All the sailors wept in gratitude and admiration for her courage and filial piety. She said a quiet prayer and then jumped into the ocean. As soon as the ocean engulfed her, the violent waters became calm. As she sank deeper into the cold ocean, she saw a bright light. To her astonishment, she found that she could breathe. She was brought to the Dragon King and lived happily in the underwater palace. But after a while she became homesick and longed to see her father again. The Dragon King, touched by her filial piety and selfless devotion, sent her to the world above in the form of a lotus flower. This was no ordinary lotus flower, though. The local fishermen who found it decided that it should be a gift for their king. The queen had recently passed away and the king was deeply grieved. When he saw the lotus flower, he felt that it was so beautiful that it should have its own special room. Each day, he would gaze upon it in wonder. Each night, Sim Cheong would emerge from the blossom and at dawn she would return to it.

Unable to sleep one night, the king took a walk to see the lotus flower. To his great amazement, he saw a beautiful woman. Falling in love with her instantly, he decided that she would be his bride. They lived happily, but the king sensed that his new bride was not completely happy, and so he told her he would grant any wish just to make her happy. Hoping to find her father, she asked him to hold a feast for all the blind men in the country. Although it seemed a strange wish, the king granted it. At the feast, the new queen scoured the invited guests to see whether her father was among them. Just as the feast was about to end, a blind beggar showed up at the gates. It was the queen's father. "Father! Father!" she shouted. Upon hearing his daughter's voice, old man Sim opened his eyes wide, and as he did so, he realized that he could finally see. Father and daughter embraced and wept for joy.

Jingnyeo, the weaving maiden, and Gyeonu, the herder

Once upon a time, there lived a lovely princess called Jingnyeo직녀. She loved to weave and nobody in the land could weave more beautifully than she. The king was very proud of his daughter. One day he realized that she was no longer a little girl, but a lovely young maiden. He called a meeting to discuss all eligible bachelors. After a few days, one of his advisors informed the king that in the neighboring kingdom lived a prince called Gyeonu견우 who would be a perfect match for the princess. All of the advisors agreed that a herder and a weaver would make a perfect match. The king sent a high court official to the neighboring kingdom to arrange a marriage. When the neighboring king accepted the offer, an auspicious day was selected for the marriage and preparations began in earnest. The prince and the princess were finally married.

However, soon they began to neglect their duties. Jingnyeo's loom gathered dust and Gyeonu's cows wandered aimlessly. When Jingnyeo's father got word of their idleness, he became very angry, and decreed that they would live apart—Gyeonu in the east and Jingnyeo in the west.

Despite their heart-wrenching pleas, the king was adamant. Gyeonu was sent to a kingdom in the east to tend cows and Jingnyeo to a kingdom in the west to weave. However, they wept so bitterly that the king decided to let them meet once a year on the seventh day of the seventh moon by the Silvery River. The husband spent his time thinking about when he would meet his wife, while she counted the days when they could be together again. Finally, a year passed and it was time to meet. With their hearts aflutter they rushed to the Silvery River, only to find that it was so wide that they couldn't cross it or even talk to each other. Without a bridge or a boat to bring them together, all they could do was stare at each other and weep. They wept so much that their tears fell to earth as rain, which turned into a flood. In order to stop the flood, the birds and animals on earth decided they had to work fast to build a bridge for the lovers.

As soon as the bridge of feathers was completed, Gyeonu and Jingnyeo rushed to each other and spent the night together. At dawn, they shed more tears and returned to their respective homes in the east and west. From that time on, magpies and crows have not been seen on the seventh day of the seventh moon, and there is always a light sprinkling of rain in the early morning of the seventh day of the seventh moon, as the tears of the lovers wet the earth.

In the West, Gyeonu and Jingnyeo are known as the bright stars Altair and Vega and the Silvery River as the Milky Way. On the seventh day of the seventh moon, the two stars are visible directly overhead on each side of the Milky Way.

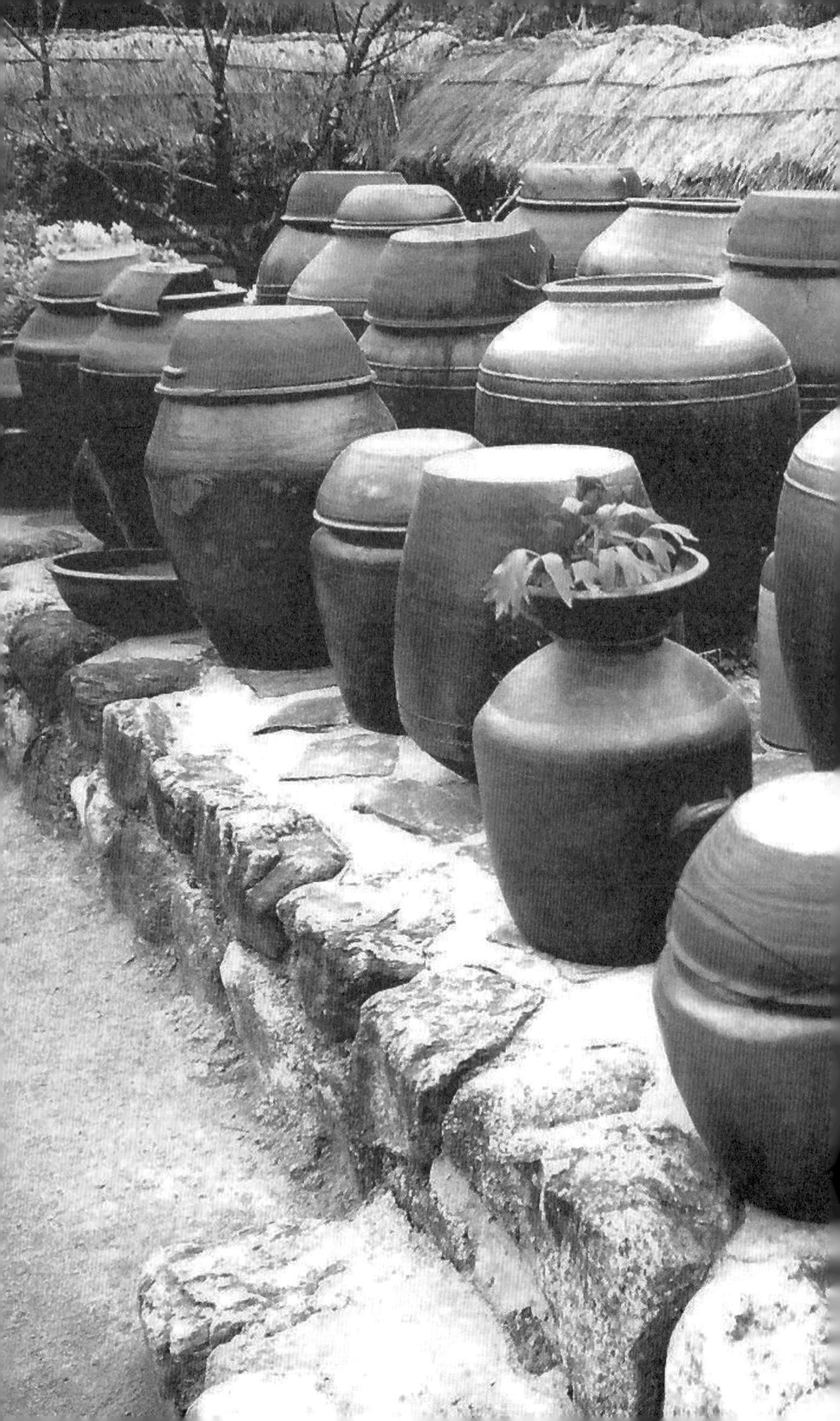

PART 3

A Glimpse of Korean Kitchen
: from the Special Occasion to the Routine

The Source of Korean's Energy
Rice

One of the great things about Korea is the food. Ordinary meals that are eaten each day are very healthy, with lots of vegetables and an all-round balanced nutrition.

A common meal consists of a bowl of rice, soup or stew, a main dish—usually either fish or meat—and smaller side dishes. Westerners who are taught that it is good manners to eat everything on their plate sometimes mistakenly think that they have to eat everything on the table, including all the side dishes. (There is also a tale of a Westerner alone at a Korean restaurant in Paris, polishing off each side dish one after another, and stacking his dishes in the process!) The side dishes complement the other dishes. At home, the same side dishes will be served for several meals until everybody gets sick of them!

The bowl of rice is the mainstay of any Korean meal. In fact, Koreans do not feel that they have finished their meal unless they have a bowl of rice. At fancier restaurants, the meal will often be served in several courses, but then at the very end, the waitress will ask (literally), "What would you like for your meal?" If this is literally interpreted, the foreigners are often astonished, thinking, "Haven't I been eating my meal?" Though Koreans are becoming more and more Westernized and rice consumption is declining, rice still plays a fundamental role in Korean cuisine. It is almost unthinkable to have a meal without rice. The rice bowl is placed to the left and the soup bowl to the right, with all the side

[bap] 밥

dishes in front. The right hand is used to manipulate the spoon and chopsticks but they should not be held in the same hand together. One usually begins by tasting the soup, taking a mouthful of rice and then some side dishes. Unlike in China and Japan, it is acceptable to use your spoon to eat the rice. If you're eating with other people, you should wait until the eldest person begins to eat before you do so.

When is rice not rice?
While in English, the word "rice" is used for all stages of its production, in Korean there is a different word for each stage.
- *monaegi* 모내기 rice planting
- *byeo* 벼 rice plant
- *ssal* 쌀 uncooked rice
- *bap* 밥 cooked rice

One of the World's Most Healthful Foods
Kimchi

What would Korean cuisine be without kimchi 김치?

Any mention of Korean cuisine must certainly include it.

Koreans like to boast about the variety of their kimchi, in a similar way that the French like to boast about the variety of their cheeses. It can virtually be made of any ingredient, from the mainstream Korean cabbage to sesame seed leaves and eggplant, and can be either spicy or mild. For Koreans, kimchi is the essence of being Korean. It is where they get their energy and dynamism, so a meal is not complete without it. In fact, when Koreans first went to Europe and there was no kimchi to be found, they used the German sauerkraut to make kimchi stew. Apparently, with a little bit of hot pepper sauce, it became relatively close to their beloved dish, as sauerkraut is also fermented.

Korean cabbage is harvested at the end of fall and right before winter starts in earnest. It is also when women begin preparing *gimjang* 김장, the pickling of kimchi for winter. It is supposed to last until the spring and traditionally was buried underground, as the ground provided natural refrigeration. Today, since so many Koreans live in apartments, it is impossible to bury the *gimjang* underground. Instead, Koreans use kimchi refrigerators which keep the temperature consistent to maximize the taste.

[gimchi] 김치

In March 2006, the American magazine *Health* named kimchi one of the world's five healthiest foods. The list included yogurt, olive oil, lentils and soy. In fact, when SARS (Severe Acute Respiratory Syndrome) broke out across Asia in 2003, Korea was unaffected, and many said that it was because of the Korean diet of kimchi, which helped stave off SARS. This had the consequence of boosting kimchi exports to other Asian countries.

As with yogurt and other fermented foods, the benefits of kimchi are found in the lactic acid bacteria (lactobacilli). These bacteria stimulate digestion and, according to many, boost immunity. They are also believed to help stop and prevent yeast infections. The vegetables provide ample vitamins (A, B and C) and antioxidants, which help protect cells from carcinogens. The high fiber content in it also helps bowel movements.

Any downsides? First and foremost, the smell. Because it contains lots of garlic, it has a very pungent smell which lingers. (If you plan to eat kimchi, make sure that your better half also has some!) Also, if you eat too much of it, it could lead to gastric cancer. The fact that it is marinated in brine before it is mixed with other spices also makes it a salty dish, though less so compared to the past, since kimchi refrigerators are now available and Koreans have become more aware of the danger of salty foods. All in all, however, the benefits of kimchi greatly outweigh the disadvantages.

Say Kimchi!
Instead of saying "cheese" when taking pictures, Koreans often say "kimchi 김치."

Everything about Kimchi

Making kimchi pancakes

Making kimchi 김치 is extremely labor-intensive and not guaranteed to be a success. Even in Korea, many young married women get their kimchi supply either from their mother, their mother-in-law or from a supermarket.

If you live in a major town or city there is bound to be a Korean supermarket—in the US for certain, but also in many European cities.

Therefore instead of making the kimchi itself, here is a quick and easy recipe that only requires kimchi that you can buy.

INGREDIENTS   1 cup of kimchi
              2 cups of flour
              Water (squid optional)

DIRECTIONS

1. Chop kimchi into thin slices about 1-2cm wide.
2. Make a flour batter. The consistency should be slightly watery.
3. Combine the kimchi slices with the flour batter and make sure that it is well mixed.
4. Oil and heat frying pan.
5. Spread mixture in the frying pan and cook until it becomes slightly brown on both sides.
6. Enjoy!

※ Note: Kimchi pancakes are especially great on a rainy day with a glass of *makgeolli* 막걸리!

The most common types of kimchi

Baechu kimchi 배추김치 Whole cabbage kimchi
When you say "kimchi," this is the kimchi that most people think of, the classic so to speak. It is usually eaten as a side dish, and when it ferments further and becomes too sour, it is used as an ingredient for kimchi stew and kimchi pancakes.

Baek kimchi 백김치 White cabbage kimchi
Baek kimchi originally came from North Korea, where less salt and red pepper are used in cooking. Essentially the same as whole cabbage kimchi, but without the red pepper, making it easier to swallow. Children often like this type of kimchi.

Bossam kimchi 보쌈김치 Rolled kimchi
The "royal" kimchi, so to speak, is called *bossam* kimchi, which means wrap. Numerous ingredients that are not usually found in ordinary kimchi such as oysters, octopus, Korean pears, chestnuts, pine nuts, jujubes and red pepper threads ensure that this is the Rolls Royce of kimchi. It is extremely labor-intensive because each wrap must be prepared individually.

Chonggak kimchi 총각김치 Ponytail kimchi
In ancient times, young men and women wore their hair in braids until they were married. Because the long radish resembles the long braided ponytail, this kimchi is called, literally, young man's kimchi.

Dongchimi 동치미 Winter white water kimchi
Considered a delicacy to be enjoyed during the winter, *dongchimi* is best served when its juice is slightly frozen. The tasty kimchi juice is even used as a noodle soup base in the winter.

The Older the Better
Fermented Foods

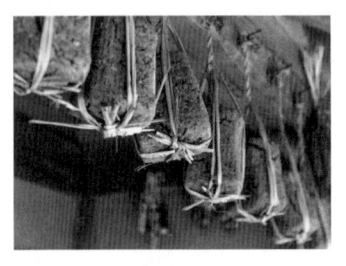

There are two pastes that form the basis of all spices in Korean cuisine. The first is *doenjang*된장 which is made from fermented soybeans, and the other is *gochujang*고추장 which is made from red peppers.

Doenjang, a vegetable protein, has been proven to be extremely healthful not only as an anti-carcinogenic but also in preventing obesity because of the fungus, bacteria and yeast that is formed during fermentation.

Because of its detoxifying quality, if *doenjang* soup is eaten in the morning, it cleanses the body of impurities and toxins that accumulated in the body overnight and also cleanses the blood. It is especially effective in breaking down toxins in vegetables, mushrooms, and meats and also helps expel nicotine from the body. Placing *doenjang* on a bee sting or snake bite is a favorite folk remedy for detoxifying the venom. It is also effective in preventing hypertension because it expels cholesterol in the blood and also makes the veins more elastic. Plus, because it helps digestion, it is often eaten together with meats. Finally, it is supposed to prevent senile dementia because the lecithin in the soybeans stimulates brain activity.

So, how is it eaten? The most common way is in soups or stews—soups with Korean cabbage, spinach or almost any kind of vegetable and stews with tofu, as well as various vegetables. It is also used as a sauce for herbs and mixed together with *gochujang*, as a vegetable dip.

된장 [doenjang]

Gochujang is a red pepper paste that is fermented and stored for consumption all year round. It also has a lot of nutrients, ranging from proteins to vitamins B2 and C to carotene. The various microorganisms together with the capsaicin in the peppers stimulate perspiration, which helps to expel toxins from the body and therefore is effective in preventing colds and other diseases. Recently, a study showed that *gochujang* also helps to prevent obesity because the capsaicin which gives the hot taste to peppers not only reduces fat, but the soybeans in it, the other main ingredient, also helps to burn off fat. In Japan, the newest diet is based on red pepper flakes.

It is also used in stews, but mostly as a base ingredient. For example, mixed with vinegar and a little bit of sugar, it makes a tasty dipping sauce for *hoe* 회, or raw fish.

The Favorite Airline Food
Bibimbap

*Bibida*비비다 means "to mix together" and *bap*밥 means "a bowl of rice." *Bibimbap*비빔밥 essentially means to mix everything together with rice, but usually at restaurants if you order *bibimbap*, you will get a variety of vegetables placed artistically on top of the rice. It is then mixed with *gochujang*고추장 sauce to make it spicy. It's up to you to determine how spicy you want it.

There are several varieties of this rice dish such as raw meat *bibimbap*, wild herbs *bibimbap* and homemade *bibimbap*, which is basically a mishmash of any leftovers. Since it was first served on Korean Air in 1990, it has gained popularity among foreigners as well. It gained even greater fame when Michael Jackson only wanted to eat *bibimbap* during his 1998 visit.

비빔밥 [bibimbap]

How to make *bibimbap*

INGREDIENTS

2 cups of rice (serves 4), 3 oz of beef, 5 dried *shiitake* mushrooms, 1 cucumber, 1/2 carrot, 2 eggs, 4 leaves of red leaf lettuce, *gochujang*

SEASONING

1 Tbs sesame seed oil, 1/2 Tbs salted sesame seeds, 1 tsp finely chopped green onion, 1 tsp finely chopped garlic, 1/2 tsp salt, beef seasoning (bulgogi 불고기 seasoning)

DIRECTIONS

1 Cook rice in a rice cooker.
2 Season beef with beef seasoning mixture and stir-fry on a skillet. Set it aside.
3 Separate egg yolks from whites. Beat each slightly with a pair of chopsticks. Pour the yolk mixture into a skillet as though you were making a round, flat omelet. Repeat with the whites. Cut both into thin yellow and white strips. If this is too much work, fry your eggs sunny-side up, and place one on top of each serving.
4 Soak shiitake mushrooms in water for 15 minutes and clean them. Squeeze out water and cut into thin strips. Stir-fry for 1-2 minutes with a little seasoning.
5 Cut cucumber in half, and slice thinly in strips. Sprinkle with salt and leave for 5 minutes. Squeeze out the liquid. Stir-fry less than a minute over high heat with a little seasoning. Do the same for the carrots.
6 Season coarsely-torn red leaf lettuce with seasoning. Put rice in a bowl, artistically place lettuce, cucumber, beef, mushrooms and top with egg. Serve with sesame oil and *gochujang* — if the gochujang is too strong, use seasoning above or use just a little.

* If you have trouble finding *shiitake* mushrooms or any of the other ingredients you can be creative and use whatever you have in your refrigerator.

The Favorite of Foreign Visitors
Bulgogi

The perennial favorite of Koreans and foreigners alike, bulgogi 불고기 is thinly sliced beef marinated in soy sauce. Actually, it is quite easy to make. As with other Korean recipes, the methodology isn't very scientific but left to the discretion of the cook.

Whenever Koreans eat meat, it is always accompanied by various vegetables. Bulgogi is often served with Korean lettuce. So take a leaf of lettuce, add a strip of bulgogi, a touch of *gochujang* 고추장 and a clove of garlic for the more daring! Enjoy!

Making bulgogi sauce

INGREDIENTS
soy sauce, sesame oil, sugar, garlic, onions, scallions

DIRECTIONS
The key is 1/2×1/2×1/2!!
What this means is that depending on how much soy sauce you use — for example, if it is a cup of soy sauce, then you should use half a cup of sesame oil and a quarter of a cup of sugar. Add garlic, onions and scallions generously. A dash of pepper, some rice wine (or just plain wine) to get rid of any meaty smell. Other vegetables can also be added, such as mushrooms. Sprinkle some sesame seeds on top as garnish.

If you have a portable gas burner, then it can be cooked directly while eating; if you have a barbecue grill, then it is great grilled; but even a frying pan over a gas stove is fine. If you can't find thinly sliced beef, you can improvise and even marinate a steak in the sauce. Accompanied with a scoop of rice, this is a delicious alternative to plain old steak!

불고기 [bulgogi]

The Key Is in the Stew

Soups or stews are an essential part of Korean cuisine. Perhaps because rice alone is difficult to swallow, Koreans feel as if there is something lacking if there is no soup or stew, especially for breakfast. There are numerous soups and stews that form a part of the Korean cuisine, but they can broadly be categorized into two groups depending on whether they are *gochujang*고추장-based or *doenjang*된장-based. The two most basic types of stew are kimchi stew and *doenjang* stew.

How to cook ham stew

INGREDIENTS

3 cups of beef stock, 4 oz of sausage, 4 oz of ham, 4 oz of bacon, 4 oz of beef, 1 bell pepper, 1 onion, 1 carrot, 1/4 of cabbage, 5 green onion, 3 oz of pasta noodles

SEASONING

2 Tbs of ground red pepper, 2 Tbs of red bean paste, 1/2 Tbs of chopped garlic, 1/2 Tbs of chopped ginger, 1 Tbs of soy sauce for soup, salt, ground black pepper

DIRECTIONS

1 Cook pasta noodles in a pot with oil and salt until al dente and drain them.
2 Cut ham, sausage, beef and bacon in bite size.
3 Dice each vegetable (carrot, cabbage, bell pepper and onion). Cut green onion into 2 inch length pieces.
4 Make seasoning.
3 Place all the meat and vegetables in a wok. Pour 3 cups of beef stock, then add seasoning on top and boil.

[jjigae] 찌개

When You Need a Boost of Energy
Samgyetang

*Samgyetang*삼계탕 literally means "ginseng, chicken, soup." To prepare, stuff a small whole chicken with ginseng, gingko nuts, garlic, dates, chestnuts and sticky rice. Let it simmer for a long time. It is enjoyed all year round but especially during the hot summer months as a way to build stamina.

During the "dog days of summer," long lines form in front of *samgyetang* restaurants with people who prefer chicken to dog meat. Naturally, those who take the term "dog-days" literally, head for those restaurants.

A side note about dog meat which is controversial in the West... dog meat is not eaten by everybody. There are those who love it and others who will not eat it even if you pay them. Special dogs are raised—just like cows or pigs—for their meat. Many in Korea now enjoy raising dogs as pets and are just as against eating dog meat as Westerners.

> **Dog days of summer**
> The dog days are the hottest days of summer. Today, with electric fans and air conditioners, it is easier to escape the summer heat. Refrigerators also make it relatively easy to prevent food from going bad. But in the past, that was difficult. Since Korean summers are especially humid, during the 20-30 days of intense summer heat, housewives took special care to make sure food didn't go bad. The dog days are divided into the "early," "middle" and "late" dog days, the period between each lasting ten to fifteen days.

[samgyetang]

Traditionally, dog meat was (and still is to some extent) eaten during the summer to combat the heat, especially during the dog days. Dog meat is believed to be easier to digest than beef, pork or even chicken and very low in cholesterol. It is also high in protein and low in fat. As proteins break down into amino acids to be absorbed by the body, the amino acids from dog meat are most similar to that of humans and, therefore, easily absorbed. For this reason, it is sometimes given to patients recovering from an illness or surgery because of its nutritional value.

For those who are adverse to dog meat and there are many in Korea who are a delicious alternative is *samgyetang*.

Korean's Favorite Noodles
Japchae

*Japchae*잡채 is a party favorite loved by young and old alike, but more by women than men. It is made of glass noodles together with carrots, onions, spinach and beef. It can even be a mish-mash of anything that's in the refrigerator. Also it can be eaten with rice as a side dish or without.

How to cook *japchae*

INGREDIENTS
12 oz of glass noodles (*dangmyeon*당면) for 4 servings, 4 oz of beef, 5 *shiitake* mushrooms, 1 carrot, 1 onion, 1 egg, spinach (a bunch), 5 Tbs of oil, salt, sesame seed oil, sesame seeds

SEASONING
2 Tbs of soy sauce, 1 Tbs of sugar, 1 Tbs of garlic, 1 Tbs of sesame seed oil, 1 Tbs of chopped green onion, ground black pepper

DIRECTIONS
1. Soak the glass noodles in hot water for about 30 minutes. For a quicker result, parboil for about 5 minutes.
2. Soak *shiitake* mushrooms in water for 15 minutes and cut off the stems. Cut each mushroom into thin strips (julienne). Cut beef into thin strips.
3. Mix all the ingredients for seasoning and marinate the beef and mushrooms in the same bowl.
4. Meanwhile, cut the carrot and the onion into thin strips.
5. In boiling water, parboil the spinach for about 2 minutes, then cool under running water. Squeeze out any remaining liquid. Season with salt and sesame seed oil.
6. Separate egg white and yolk, stir slightly with chopsticks and fry separately on a skillet. Let cool and then julienne. (An easier way is to mix the whites and yolks together and fry as directed.)
7. In a large deep pan, start cooking the beef and mushrooms with oil. When the beef is cooked, add the carrots, onions, spinach and noodles.

8 Stir-fry until all the vegetables are well cooked. Add a little bit of sesame seed oil before turning off the heat.
9 Place the *japchae* on a dish, and sprinkle egg strips and sesame seeds on top as a final touch.

* Can be served with rice for a meal or alone as an appetizer.

[japchae] 잡채

Something to Snack on

There is a variety of Korean snacks that young and old alike enjoy. The most typical snack is called *tteokbokki*떡볶이 and consists of finger-size rice cakes sautéed in *gochujang*고추장. Needless to say, it is a spicy dish. It can be found at street stalls or snack shops. So it's basically available wherever you go in Korea.

Another favorite snack is *ramyeon*라면 (noodles), something that is also found in many Western countries now. Quick to make, there are specialty shops that serve variations of *ramyeon*—with cheese, curry, tuna—or the run-of-the-mill variety can be found in any snack shop. Although dozens of different *ramyeon* can be found in supermarkets, the Korean variety tends to be hotter than the Japanese variety.

*Gimbap*김밥 is a handy snack or sometimes a meal in itself. It consists of rice wrapped in sea laver (dried seaweed) with carrots, spinach, ham and eggs. The other types of *gimbap* contain kimchi김치, tuna, beef and other fillings, and can be bought in specialty shops or in snack shops. Some people even like to eat *ramyeon* with a roll of *gimbap*. Remember, Koreans don't feel as if they've eaten properly unless they've put some rice in their stomach!

분식 [bunsik]

Bread is to the West What *Tteok* is to Korea

Rice cakes hold a special place in Korean cuisine. As an indispensable part of any festivity, there is a special kind of rice cake to fit very occasion. For example, on one's first birthday—*dol*돌, the rainbow rice cake, so-called because of its colorful layers, is supposed to be eaten by at least 100 people to ensure the baby's prosperity.

Beautifully shaped rice cakes can be quite filling and substitute as a quick meal. They also make for beautiful gifts—for holidays or important events, rice cakes are often offered as presents. On returning from their honeymoon, newlyweds will often give rice cakes as a token of their gratitude to their friends and relatives.

When opening a new business, moving into a new house or beginning something new, *sirutteok*시루떡, which consists of layers of rice cake covered with red beans, is usually served.

떡
[tteok]

Straight from the Ground to Medicine Cabinet
Korean Ginseng

Korean ginseng, a medicinal herb, is said to differ with ginseng grown in other countries. Thanks to the micro-ginsenosides found only in Korean red ginseng, Korean ginseng works in various ways to suppress cancerous cell proliferation and helps cancerous cells revert to normal ones. It helps to maintain overall physical health and vitality.

Though it is grown on ginseng farms, from time to time, wild ginseng roots are found deep in mountains. In such cases, they fetch exorbitant prices, sometimes reaching tens of thousands of dollars for one root. The more it resembles the shape of a human, the more expensive it is.

There are different ways to categorize ginseng, the most widely used criteria being age—3-to 4-year-old ginseng and 5-to 6-year-old ginseng. Naturally, the older the ginseng, the better it is.

Fresh ginseng is sometimes eaten as an appetizer at expensive restaurants, in which case they are usually small, young roots. Ginseng can be taken as a tea after it has been made into granules. In other cases, ginseng extract—a thick, molasses-like substance—can be mixed with a little bit of water. Those who don't like the slightly bitter taste but want to benefit from its healthful properties can take ginseng capsules.

고려인삼 [goryeo insam]

Enjoy a Cup of Tea!

Thanks to abundant potable water, tea was not an absolute necessity in Korea as it was in China, where clay soil abounds, or Japan, an island country. Nevertheless, in Korea, tea developed as a means to clear one's mind during meditation, among other things.

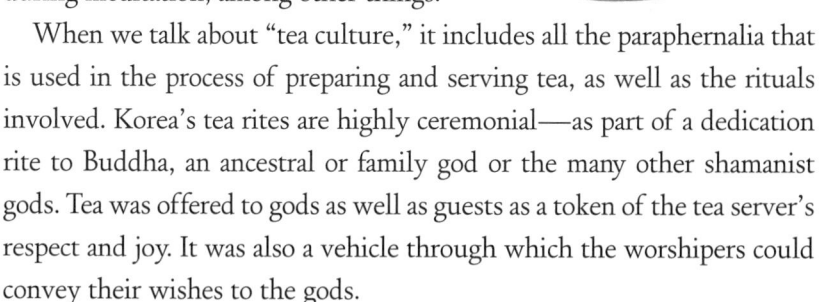

When we talk about "tea culture," it includes all the paraphernalia that is used in the process of preparing and serving tea, as well as the rituals involved. Korea's tea rites are highly ceremonial—as part of a dedication rite to Buddha, an ancestral or family god or the many other shamanist gods. Tea was offered to gods as well as guests as a token of the tea server's respect and joy. It was also a vehicle through which the worshipers could convey their wishes to the gods.

During the Joseon 조선 Dynasty (1392-1910), tea was used both for the "day tea ritual" and the "special tea ritual" by the royal family and noblemen—a distinction that is not found in other countries. For example, tea was an important part of the ritual to announce the queen or crown prince, and even to commemorate a prince's birthday. Toward the end of the Joseon Dynasty, commoners also began to use tea for their own ancestral rites.

Confucian scholars used tea as a way to develop mental discipline and self-discipline. In fact, it was said that "a cup of tea is the beginning of Zen." So when a monk says "have some tea before you go," it actually

[cha munhwa] 차문화

means "drink tea and reach enlightenment on your own" because the tea ceremony is considered by monks to be a disciplinary measure to purify the mind. Commoners also believed that tea helped to alleviate loneliness and soothe aching souls. By providing comfort in everyday life, tea was helpful in finding Truth of life.

Mogwacha 모과차 Chinese quince or papaya tea

Chinese quince is shaped like an elongated ball. It is sweet and very fragrant. Rarely eaten like other fruit in Korea, it is usually "eaten" after steeping it as tea. Thanks to its warmth, it reduces excessive body moisture and is thought to ease pain. An effective cold remedy, it is especially enjoyed when the seasons are changing. It is also particularly helpful for sore throats. Chinese quince tea is not simply a beverage; it has long been used as a remedy for sicknesses.

Yulmucha 율무차 Adlay tea

A member of the Poaceae family, adlay is rich in proteins, fat and other various nutrients. It is also known to be good for people who are dieting. Adlay tea is usually made from adlay and roasted on a weak fire: the roasted adlay is brewed up to make tea, and can be served hot or cold. Served cold, this sweet tasting tea is most enjoyed during the summer's hottest months.

Saenggangcha 생강차 Ginger tea

It is not very difficult to make ginger tea. Carefully wash some ginger under running water, then slice it or shred it. Put the prepared ginger, along with some honey, in a glass jar or an airtight container, and store it for two or three days. Later, put one or two teaspoons of ginger tea in a cup and pour boiling water over it before serving. Ginger naturally tastes spicy, so depending on personal tastes it is necessary to control the amount of water so that it is not too spicy. Also, ginger tea helps relieve hangovers, freshens your breath and is helpful as a cold remedy.

Korean Alcohol
Soju and *Makgeolli*

Wine is to France what vodka is to Russia and what tequila is to Mexico. For Korea, the most common form of alcohol is *soju*소주, which means "burning alcohol." *Soju* is usually drunk in small shot glasses and downed in a single gulp. For women, it can also be used as a cocktail base and mixed with lemon juice or cucumbers to attenuate the kick a little. Made mainly from sweet potatoes, it is usually 20 proof.

There are also many kinds of traditional rice wines, such as *makgeolli*막걸리 and *dongdongju*동동주, as well as a variety of fruit-based wines. They do not have as much punch as Chinese alcohol and are less refined than Japanese drinks. Korean traditional alcohol has a mild flavor that goes down smoothly.

Dos and don'ts of drinking in Korea
- It is considered unseemly to drink alone. Koreans like to drink together and in large groups, and will take turns drinking from the same cup to build harmony.
- If someone pours a drink for you, you should return the favor. However, wait until they've finished their drink.
- It is considered inconsiderate if your drinking partner has to pour his own drink. Your partner might even joke, "Are you busy?" meaning, "Can't you see that my glass is empty?"
- Be sure that the glass is empty before you pour more into the glass.

[sul]

Table Manners

As in all countries, Korea has its own table etiquette that should be observed. These are just a few pointers, should you be invited out for a meal in Korea.

General table manners
- Before starting to eat in earnest, begin by tasting the soup or kimchi juice.
- Do not lift your rice or soup bowl.
- Begin eating your rice and side dishes from one side or not from the middle.
- Do not use your fingers to eat.
- Make sure your utensils do not hit the dishes or make a noise.
- Do not eat with your mouth open and do not make noise while eating.
- When you have finished eating, return your utensils to the position they were when you started eating.

Manners when eating with elders
- The elder should be seated away from the door.
- Wait to begin after the elder has lifted his/her utensils.
- If you finish eating before the elder, place your utensils in the rice or soup bowl. After the elder has finished, place it on the table.

식사예절 [siksa yejeol]

Proper use of utensils

- Do not hold your spoon and chopsticks in the same hand.
- Do not lick your spoon.
- When using your chopsticks, place the spoon on the table.
- Do not place your spoon or chopsticks on any of the side dishes.
- Use your spoon for stews or other side dishes that contain liquid, or else use your chopsticks.

Hansang

Some restaurants do not have a separate menu, from which you can order individual dishes. Rather, they have "set menus" for which you choose one for everybody. In this case, you will be sitting on the floor in a room with no table in sight. After you order, the waitresses will carry in the table laden with food. The requisite rice and soup will be present together with more dishes than you can count. They will usually consist of grilled fish, beef — usually bulgogi불고기 — together with different herbs, kimchi김치 and other side dishes, creating an impressive spread.

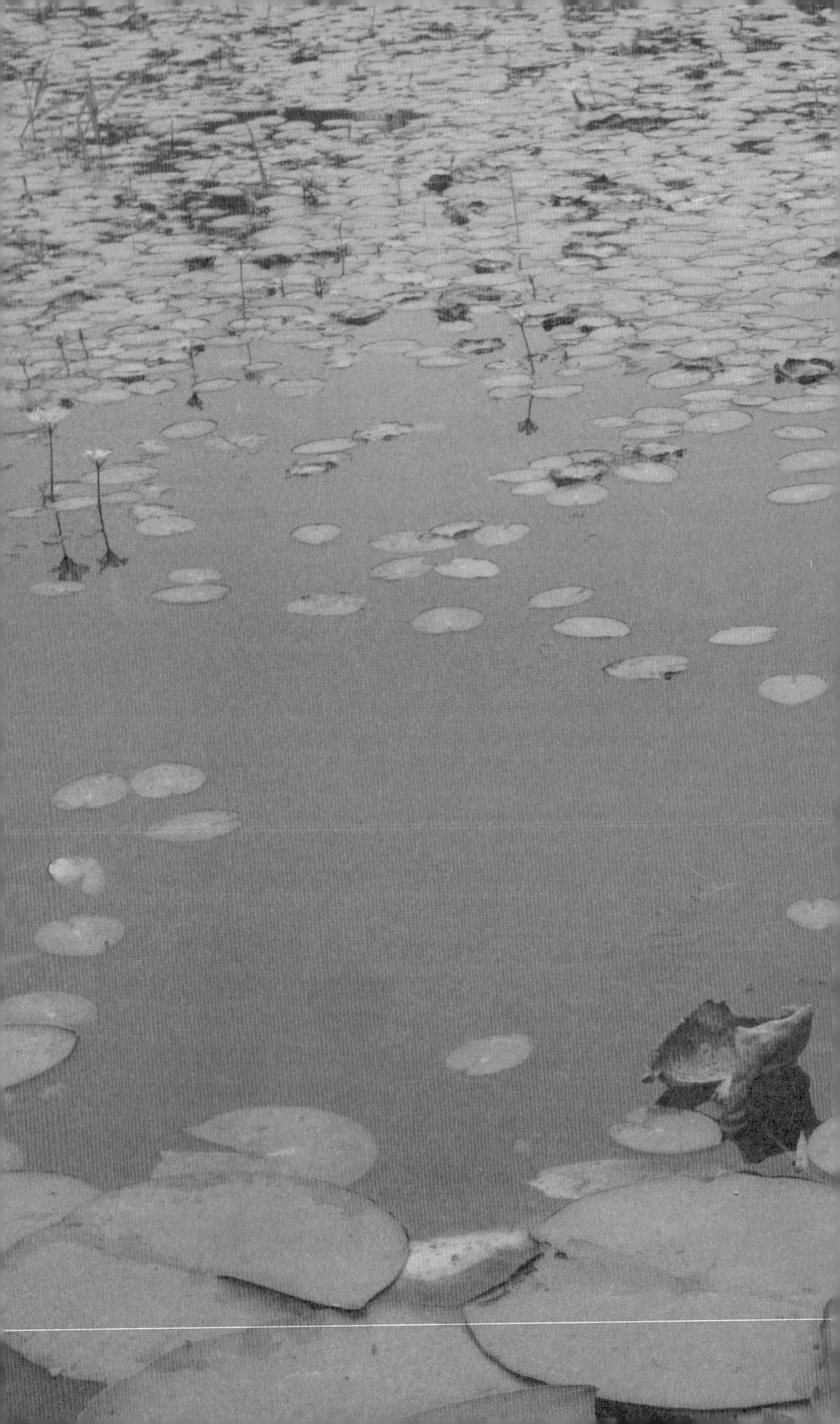

PART 4

A Guide for Armchair Travelers
: Spots and Places

Breathing Life into Seoul
The Hangang River

All major cities developed around rivers and Seoul is no exception. Though the Hangang River한강 is not that long (514km), the southern portion is particularly wide (more than one kilometer in some areas). As a result, there are 25 bridges that link the south and north sides of the river.

The economic boom that Korea enjoyed from the 1960s up until the 1980s has often been dubbed "The Miracle on the Hangang River." Since the 1980s, spurred by the 1988 Seoul Olympic Games, the government has made a conscious effort to beautify and develop the riverside. A 41.5km area was developed to accommodate green areas, water skiing, yachting and boating facilities, fishing spots and sports facilities such as soccer fields, volleyball courts, basketball courts and swimming pools.

There is also a cruise boat plying the entire length of the river, and passengers can get on and off at stops along the way. While there are no particular sights along the river, it is an interesting boat ride, especially at night.

The Hangang embankment is a popular spot for couples because of the parks, the night lights and the cruise ship. During the hot summer months, in particular, families flock to this area to cool themselves in the fresh river breeze.

[han-gang] 한강

Royal Palaces

With a long history of royalty, Seoul is dotted with numerous royal palaces. In fact, Seoul was the capital city of the Joseon 조선 Dynasty, which lasted from 1392 to 1910. Step into a few palaces and experience the calm and tranquility of years past.

Gyeongbokgung Palace

Completed in 1395, this was the residence of the founder of the Joseon Dynasty. Meaning "shining happiness," Gyeongbokgung 경복궁 Palace was meant to bring everlasting happiness and prosperity to Korea's kings, their descendants and the people. This palace was burnt down during the 1592 Japanese invasion, but was rebuilt in 1865. It was again demolished during Japanese colonial rule (1910-1945). However, thanks to government efforts, it has now been restored to its original state.

The main gate of this palace is called Gwanghwamun 광화문, which is also the name of the neighborhood. It is guarded by two large *haetae* 해태, a mythical animal that was believed to use its horns to punish evildoers. The *haetae* stand tall to ensure that government officials remain honest.

Changdeokgung Palace

Also known as the Secret Garden, this palace is the best preserved palace in Seoul. It was designated as a world heritage site by UNESCO in 1997. Considered an auspicious site, King Taejong 태종 ordered construction of a new palace in the early 15th century. The result was a complex composed of official and residential buildings, with a garden that did not change or

고궁 [gogung]

mar the natural topography but rather embraced it. Consequently, this palace is not only a prime example of Korean palace architecture and design, but also the philosophy of Koreans to embrace and blend in with nature.

Unlike other palaces, only guided tours are allowed in this palace, which are offered in English, Japanese, Chinese and Korean. The changing of the guards' ceremony is also held here. See it and compare it with that of Buckingham Palace! Every fall, around October, a parade of royal carriages and a reenactment of the civil service examination can be seen.

The National Museum of Korea

Reopened in October 2005, the more than 150,000 historical relics and artifacts are housed in this modern, environmentally-friendly environment to ensure optimum conditions for preservation. The digital guides (PDA) and audio guides (MP3) provide explanations of the artifacts to ensure that visitors understand the history behind the displays. The exhibits consist of cultural properties from all over the country and spanning all the ages. The museum presents the history and culture of Korea in a nutshell.

Catching a Glimpse of Life in the Past
Traditional Villages

Due to breakneck economic development and urbanization, many neighborhoods with traditional Korean houses have been virtually wiped off the map. There are, however, some pockets that have been preserved. Here are just a few of those unscathed or restored areas.

Namsangol Hanok Village

Smack in the heart of Seoul, where you least expect it, you can find Namsangol Hanok 남산골 한옥 Village. If you only have a few hours in Seoul and want to get a feel for how Koreans lived centuries ago, or if there's no time to visit a larger folk village, the Namsangol is the perfect solution. This village is a recreation of five traditional Korean houses, a pavilion, a pond and a time capsule. As you enter the front gate, you will see a large area where various outdoor performances are held. If you walk a little further into the village you will see five traditional houses built in the Joseon 조선 Dynasty style. These houses showcase the various social ranks of society from peasant to king. The furniture is also arranged so that visitors can see how Koreans lived in the past.

After a walk around the village, you can enjoy traditional tea and refreshments. There are also traditional games that you can try out, such as sea-saw jumping, arrow throwing and *yunnori* 윷놀이. If you're lucky, you

민속촌 [minsokchon]

can also catch a reenactment of a traditional marriage ceremony. You can also try on the traditional bride and groom costume and take some photos.

Walking further will take you to a very modern looking monument. This time capsule was buried in 1994 to commemorate Seoul's 600th anniversary as the capital of this country. It will be opened again on its millennium anniversary in 2994. One of the strong points of this village is that you can really feel the four distinct seasons of Korea.

Hahoe Folk Village

If you want to be transported back in time, take a trip to Hahoe Folk Village 하회마을. Though you will see peeks of modernity here and there, for the most part the traditions and ways of life of hundreds of years ago have been preserved in this folk village. People still actually live there, so there is less of a sense of artificiality. The reason it is so well-preserved is because it is surrounded by mountains and rivers. Today it is a favorite film location for historical dramas and documentaries. If possible, try to visit on a weekday because tourists flock there on weekends and holidays, and it's nearly impossible to feel a sense of times past.

Dating back to the Goryeo 고려 period (918-1392), this village is unique because both the *yangban* 양반 (aristocrats) and commoners lived in the same village. The layout is concentric, with the upper class houses in the center and the lower class ones on the outer bounds of the village. Another difference is that from the center of the village, all the houses face different directions, unlike most Korean houses, which tend to face south (see Part 5 for *hanok*).

Before entering the village, you can visit the Hahoe 하회 Mask Museum, where hundreds of Korean masks and masks from cultures around the world are on display. The Hahoe mask dance which combines masks, dance, drama and shamanic rituals, was designated Important Intangible Cultural Asset No. 69. Using humor and satire, it makes light of the tensions between social classes and can be understood by everyone regardless of their nationality.

At the entrance of the village you will see a large collection of *jangseung* 장승, objects that look similar to totem poles. These are carved wooden statues which were used to protect the village against evil spirits. They usually stand in pairs at the village entrance; the one on the left is supposed to ward off the heavenly spirits; the one on the right, the earth spirits. Often there is a male and female *jangseung* as well.

The Korean Folk Village

Opened in October 1974, the Korean Folk Village was created as an open-air folk museum to attract international tourists as well as domestic visitors. Thanks to its proximity to Seoul—it takes about one hour from Seoul, depending on traffic—it is one of the most visited folk villages.

The marketplace is quite interesting and there are numerous shops selling handicrafts that are made right on the grounds. Twice a day, farmers' music and dance as well as tightrope acrobatics are performed, and initiation rites such as coming-of-age ceremonies, marriages, funerals and ancestral memorials are recreated.

You should plan to be there for at least a full day, as there is much to see. Over 260 traditional houses have been built in the late-Joseon Dynasty style, and you'll get a glimpse of the food, clothing and styles of long ago. There are a dozen workshops specializing in various handicrafts such as pottery, basket and bamboo weaving, rice paper making, and other arts. Or enjoy watching master craftsmen and women create beautiful designs in brass, embroidery, iron and clay.

Because it is a re-creation of Korea's past, the village does an excellent job of showing the regional variations of housing styles. There are houses from the colder northern region and some from the warmer southern region, as well as from Jejudo 제주도, the volcanic island, off Korea's southern coast. In addition, you can also see the social strata of Korea's past society through the houses of poor farmers, rich farmers, the *yangban* class, a shaman's house, a Confucian academy and a magistrate's office.

Housing a Feat in Printing History
Haeinsa Temple

Haeinsa해인사 Temple is located at the southwestern foot of Mt. Gayasan가야산, in the southeastern part of the Korean peninsula. The name derives from a phrase from a Buddhist scripture and means "true figures of the universe are revealed as they are." Built in AD 802, this temple is one of the three Jewel Temples of Buddhism in Korea. This temple charms tourists with its strange rocks and cliffs, its clear water throughout the valleys, and its dense, beautiful forest of fine trees around the area. Also, Jikjisa직지사 Temple, Hapcheon합천 Dam, and Geochang거창 Hot Springs are located nearby, making it a true tourist attraction. Yet what makes this temple most famous is the Buddhist scriptures kept here.

The Tripitaka Koreana, known as *Palman daejanggyeong*팔만대장경 in Korean, is the most complete collection of Buddhist scriptures, laws and treatises. It was engraved on more than 80,000 woodblocks between 1237 and 1248. The 81,340 blocks weigh 3.2kg each and are the equivalent of 6,791 printed volumes. The storage buildings (*Janggyeong panjeon*장경판전 Hall) to house the woodblocks are themselves considered to be outstanding works of art, and indicate an amazing knowledge of preservation techniques.

해인사 [haeinsa]

History

The original Tripitaka Koreana set was completed in 1087 and took 77 years to complete. After they were destroyed in 1232 during a Mongol invasion, King Gojong 고종 decreed that the set be remade in the hope that Buddha would intervene and help repel any subsequent Mongolian attacks.

Process

The Buddhist monks used the wood of silver magnolias, white birches and cherry trees growing on the southern coast. The wood was soaked in brine for three years before it was cut into individual blocks. Each section was again boiled in brine and dried before being carved.

The dedication and self-discipline that allowed monks to make no mistakes, no deviations, in creating the Tripitaka Koreana is something that people today cannot fathom. Furthermore, it is said that the monks bowed each time they wrote a character. As a result of such earnest work, the text, which was written by more than 30 people, still comes across as if the magnificent work of a single person.

Storage

When one considers that the blocks were made of wood, it is amazing that they were able to survive 750 years! This was possible thanks to the storage halls where they are housed, which consist of foundations insulated with charcoal, lime powder and clay, and which help to maintain a constant temperature and humidity level.

Korean Buddhism and
Buddhist Temples

Before Buddhism was introduced to Korea via China in 372, the native religion was shamanism. Since Buddhism did not clash with shamanist philosophies, the two blended well. For example, according to shamanist beliefs, mountains were the home of mountain spirits yet they became the sites for Buddhist temples. Another way the two religions blended was in the spirits that were revered. In Korean shamanism, the three main spirits are the mountain spirit, *sansin*산신, the recluse, *dokseong*독성, and the spirit of the seven stars, *chilseong*칠성. Korean Buddhism, even today, has special shrines for these three spirits in its temples.

Besides the basic fundamental teachings of the Buddha, Korean Buddhism evolved from this blend of Buddhism and shamanism. Korean Buddhism was widely accepted, even becoming the state ideology during the Goryeo고려 period and of the Silla신라 Kingdom. Later, though, it experienced extreme repression during the Joseon조선 Dynasty, when neo-Confucian ideology gained primacy. However, thanks to the help of Buddhist monks during the Japanese invasion led by Toyotomi Hideyoshi toward the end of the 16th century, persecution of Buddhism came to a halt. It kept a relatively low profile until the Japanese occupation, at which time it gained wider acceptance. Today, about 25% of the Korean population is Buddhist, compared to 18% of the population which is Christian.

불교 [bulgyo]

Whenever you see a Korean proper noun that ends with *sa*사 you can be pretty sure that it is a temple. Korean Buddhist temples, like the religion itself, were the object of continual cycles of royal patronage, invasion and destruction, reconstruction and conflagration that all reflect the history of the country itself. As Buddhism became an integral part of Korean culture, it took on the following characteristics: first, it became a part of local culture while at the same time it boosted greater cultural achievements, as is seen by the innumerable national treasures that are Buddhist; second, Korean Buddhism blended together all types of Buddhism to become "*tongil bulgyo*통일불교," or all-inclusive Buddhism; third, Korean Buddhism is closely linked with national harmony, prosperity and protection. It is not difficult to find these three elements in temples around the nation. These distinct characteristics can be seen in the architecture, paintings and rituals of Korean Buddhism.

Many temples are located deep in the heart of mountain areas, and therefore, a visit to a temple provides an opportunity to cleanse the mind and body. Most temples have three gates through which visitors must pass in order to prepare them for the path to enlightenment. The first gate is the One Pillar Gate, signifying the unity of all things in the universe. It is followed by the Guardian Gate, where the Guardians of the Four Directions or Four Heavenly Kings—huge and angry looking guardians—stare down at you. The last gate is the Gate of Non-duality meaning that the secular world you are leaving behind and the world of Buddha that you are entering are not separate. Though each temple has its own unique configuration, influenced by history, the Buddhist sect and the purpose of the temple, a typical Korean Buddhist temple consists of the three gates, a main hall, monks' quarters, guest rooms, a kitchen, meditation, and study halls, as well as pavilions and shrines. Since the main hall is usually the first place visited, it is directly in line with the gates. Pagodas, stone lanterns, stupas, memorial steles are also found within the complex.

If possible, try to time your visit to coincide with morning or evening prayers. The prayers are characterized by continuous chanting and bowing. But before the chanting, four percussion instruments are played. This, in itself, is quite an experience.

See the Seas Divide
Jindo Island

Composed of about 250 islands and islets, Jindo진도 Island is the third-largest island in Korea, after Jejudo제주도 and Geojedo거제도 Islands. It is famous as the site of General Yi Sun-shin이순신's great naval victory, the *jindotgae*진돗개 breed of dogs and the *gugija*구기자 berry.

It is also famous for the so-called "Moses' Miracle." Around the end of February and the middle of June (of the lunar calendar), the sea "splits" in half and a dry path is formed, much like what happened in the Book of Exodus in the Old Testament. The road that is formed is about 30-40 meters wide and 2.8km long. It appears for only about one hour before being submerged again.

As with most unexplained phenomena, this one also has a legend to go along with it. The story goes that, once upon a time, there were many tigers on Jindo Island. The islanders became frightened of the frequent appearances of the tigers in their village and therefore fled to Modo모도 Island. However, Grandma Ppong뽕 was left behind. She prayed every day to the god of the ocean to reunite her with her family. Then, around February, the god of the ocean appeared in her dreams and told her that he would send a rainbow to the sea and that she was to ride it across the ocean. The following day, when she went out to the sea the seas parted and a rainbow appeared. Grandma Ppong and her family were thus reunited.

To commemorate this legend, the Yeongdeungje영등제 Festival, which includes folk plays, is held every year.

[jindo] 진도

Indigenous Korean Dogs

According to the literature, there were nine dogs indigenous to Korea, but three breeds were exterminated during the Japanese colonial rule and the Korean War. The following is a description of three breeds that still remain today:

Jindotgae
Named after Jindo 진도 Island for centuries the *jindotgae* 진돗개 breed could only be found on that island. This breed is recognized as National Treasure No. 53 and therefore, an export of the dog is prohibited.

The *jindotgae* is a medium-sized dog with a lean body, enabling it to run extremely long distances. Under Korean law, only white and red or tan-colored *jindotgae* are officially recognized, and therefore they are the most popular. It is very independent and extremely intelligent, answering only to its master. It also has a fighting spirit. There are numerous stories about how they have run thousands of kilometers to find their way back home.

The reaction of *jindotgae* 진돗개 owners is extreme—either they love them or they feel that they are too difficult to raise and never want to have one again. This is because *jindotgae* are extremely independent dogs which make them good at hunting deer, rabbits, racoons, badgers, and wild boars. They will bring small game to their master, but for larger animals, it will lead the master to the game.

Sapsalgae

Literally "the dog that roots out evil spirits," *sapsalgae* 삽살개 were recognized as an indigenous breed and designated Korean National Treasure No. 368. This native dog, which looks like a sheep dog, has long been a part of Korean history. It almost became extinct during the 35-year Japanese occupation, when the Japanese slaughtered between 300,000 to 500,000 *sapsalgae*, mostly for their fur and leather. Today, there is an active movement to preserve the breed.

There are two types of the breed—one, the blue *sapsalgae*, has black and white fur which takes on a bluish tint in the moonlight. The yellow *sapsalgae* is slightly larger and has yellow fur with black and white patches. It is a sturdy dog, resistant to the cold winters and hot summers of Korea.

Pungsangae

The *pungsangae* 풍산개 is a quiet, strong and intelligent dog. Once it sets its sights on a hunting target, it has the tenacity to stay with it until the very end. Its fur color ranges from white, yellow to light yellow-grey or black. It is quiet and well-suited as a guard dog. In North Korea, it is known as a tiger hunter. North Korea has designated it as National Treasure No. 38. Today, they are trained to chase away wild boars.

In June 2000, during the historic South-North summit meeting between North Korean Leader Kim Jong-il 김정일 and former South Korean President Kim Dae-jung 김대중, the North Korean leader gave President Kim a pair of *pungsangae* as a gift to South Korea. One was named Autonomy and the other Unification but the North Korean leader encouraged President Kim to name them as he liked. They were renamed Uri 우리 (we) and Duri 두리 (the two of us).

The Cradle of Ancient Civilization
Gyeongju

Often dubbed a "museum without walls," this ancient capital city of the Silla 신라 Kingdom is an outstanding concentration of Buddhist art and the cultural achievements of the era. The Gyeongju 경주 historical district contains prime examples of Korean Buddhist art—sculptures, reliefs, pagodas, temples and palaces, especially from the 7th to 10th centuries. As such, it was recognized as a World Heritage site by UNESCO in 2000.

To begin with, the Gyeongju National Museum is a permanent exhibit of the items excavated from the numerous royal tombs of the area, among other historical items.

The Dumulli 두물리 Park is located in the heart of Gyeongju and houses 23 royal tombs, but if you have only time to see one, then visit the Flying Horse Tomb, or Cheonmachong 천마총. It was excavated in 1974 and revealed more than 10,000 relics. The tomb is open to the public and allows visitors to see first-hand how the tombs were constructed.

Cheomseongdae 첨성대 Observatory is a stone tower that is considered as the oldest astronomical observatory in Asia. This bottle-shaped structure

경주 [gyeongju]

is composed of 365 stones and 12 rectangular base stones, with 12 levels of stones above and below the central window.

Anapji 안압지 Pond is where the royal family entertained important guests and enjoyed relaxing moments. Another prime example of how Korean gardens blend and harmonize with their natural surroundings, the pond was the repository of more than 700 historical relics.

The most famous Buddhist temple in Korea, Bulguksa 불국사, was recognized as a UNESCO World Cultural Heritage site in 1995, and considered to be a masterpiece of Korean culture. Dabotap 다보탑 and Seokgatap 석가탑 are the most famous stone pagodas dedicated to the *Sakyamuni* Buddha and the Buddha of Abundant Treasures (*Prabhutaratna*), respectively, and exemplify the desire of the people of Silla to embody Buddhist ideals in the mundane world. The highlight of the visit to Bulguksa Temple is the main Buddha at Seokguram 석굴암 Grotto, which sits serenely under the vault of the rotunda. This Buddha represents the pinnacle of stone sculpture, so lifelike that we feel we will be enlightened at any moment. Mt. Namsan 남산, just south of Gyeongju, provided the background for artists carving these Buddhas and Bodhisattvas. Any frame captured of Mt. Namsan is a painting in the making. The peaks and valleys are scattered with extraordinary relics of Silla Buddhism, thanks to which the Mt. Namsan Belt was designated as a UNESCO World Cultural Heritage site in 2001.

What to do in Gyeongju

Besides taking in all the history and culture in Gyeongju, you can enjoy some fun activities. If you go to Mt. Banwolsan반월산 horse riding farm, you can experience an exciting horse ride, even if you're a novice. Otherwise, you can try your hand at archery at Banwolseong반월성 Fortress. Korea is the undisputed champion in men's and women's archery, capturing innumerable Olympic and world championship gold, silver and bronze medals. The archery tradition dates back to the Silla era, so discover the secret for yourself!

Other traditional games, such as Korean wrestling (ssireum씨름), yunnori윷놀이, arrow throwing, or tuho투호, among others, can also be played at Banwolseong Fortress.

What to eat? Gyeongju is also famous for its beopju법주 (Korean traditional alcohol), which is produced by Grandma Bae배, who has been designated an Intangible Cultural Asset for her distilling skills.

Hwangnamppang황남빵 bread is a sweet bread filled with red bean paste that is still made using hand-held scales to weigh the water and wheat flour. No artificial sweeteners or preservatives are used. Haejangguk해장국 is a soup that will cure any hangover thanks to the plentiful bean sprouts in the soup, but it can also be enjoyed sober!

Bulguksa legend

Legend has it that Kim Dae-seong김대성 lived with his widowed mother and eked out a living by working the fields of a wealthy landowner in his village. Through hard work, he was able to build a modest hut and buy a small plot of land. One day, a monk called Jeomgae점개 came to the village begging for alms for a large religious gathering. A man in the village promised 50 rolls of hemp cloth and in return the monk began to preach to the villagers that for every good deed, they would be repaid ten thousand times in happiness and longevity. Upon hearing this, Kim Dae-seong donated his small field but died soon after. On the very day that he died, the prime minister of Silla heard a voice from above saying that he would soon have a child who would be called Dae-seong. That evening, the prime minister's wife became pregnant and gave birth to a child with the name "Dae-seong" inscribed on his palm. The child was therefore called by that name. As a boy, he enjoyed hunting. One day, while on a hunting expedition, he stalked and killed a bear. That evening, he had a dream in which the bear's angry spirit vowed to transform itself and kill him. In return for his life, he agreed to build a temple for the bear. Thereafter, Kim Dae-seong gave up hunting and built a temple called Ungsusa웅수사 on the site where he had killed the bear. He consequently became a devout Buddhist and later built Bulguksa Temple for his parents.

The Beautiful Southern Island
Jejudo

Jejudo 제주도 is an island as close as Korea gets to a tropical climate. Throughout the year, it enjoys a mild oceanic climate and has therefore long been the honeymoon spot for Koreans. The largest of the islands surrounding Korea, it is located at the southernmost tip of the peninsula. It was formed by several volcanic eruptions. In the center of the island stands Mt. Hallasan 한라산 at 1,950m above sea level.

If you go to Jejudo, you will notice that there are three things in abundance, the so-called "three many": rocks, wind and women. There are many rocks because it is a volcanic island; there is lots of wind because it is an island; and there are lots of women because traditionally men went out to sea, never returned. Also, the women have always been very visible—not only working in the fields but also busy in the sea diving for shellfish.

There are also three things which the island has traditionally been said to lack: thieves, gates and beggars. Life on the island was not easy and so people knew that they had to be diligent, thrifty and interdependent in order to survive. And since no one stole or begged, gates became superfluous. Also, since everyone knew each other so well, it was difficult for them to do anything dishonorable. In the past, people used a log instead of a gate to let visitors know whether or not the owner was in.

제주도 [jejudo]

If you visit Jejudo after a short stay in Seoul, you will notice that it is very different from the mainland. In fact, because Jejudo used to be so isolated from the rest of the country, the culture and the dialect have evolved in a unique way. The dialect that is used on this island is very different from other dialects used across the country, which are basically simple, slight variations on word suffixes or intonation. Even today it is difficult for mainlanders to understand the Jejudo dialect. Also, Jejudo has long had a matriarchal family structure, embodied by the *haenyeo*해녀, or "sea women," who were often the heads of family, in the past.

There is plenty to see and do on Jejudo. If you go there in the spring, you will see the island awash in a sea of yellow. These are the rape flowers that bloom during the spring and cover the island. If you go during the summer, you'll find beaches full of swimmers dotting the coastline. These stretches of sand overlook waters which are quite shallow and calm. In the winter, visitors enjoy skiing, and all year round, there are extreme sports and various other activities. In the evening, there are numerous casinos that are open only to foreigners.

Hallyu in Jejudo

*Hallyu*한류, or "Korean wave," is the cultural phenomenon that is sweeping across Asia. Korean TV dramas, movies and music are gaining wide popularity. Several of the most beloved TV dramas were filmed on Jejudo Island. In March 2006, a mini theme park showcasing the TV hit *Jewel in the Palace* 대장금, opened at the Jeju제주 Folk Village. Many of the scenes in which *Jewel in the Palace*, learns the fine points of Oriental medicine were filmed at this folk village. *All In*올인 was another popular TV miniseries which was also filmed on Jejudo. The story is about a young man who makes his fortune in a casino in order to win back his true love.

Manjanggul Cave

Designated a natural monument, Manjanggul만장굴 Cave is one of the finest lava tunnels in the world. Though the cave is about 13,422 meters long, only one kilometer of the cave is open to the public. There are numerous interesting natural structures inside the cave, including 70cm long stalagmites, lava tube tunnels, stone pillar and stalactites. The formation known as Stone Turtle is interesting because it looks like Jejudo Island. Bats and other animals also reside in these tunnels, which maintain a temperature of 11-21°C.

Marado Island

Located in the southernmost area of Korea, Marado마라도 is a small island — only 4.2km long and 39m wide. Depending on the weather, a ferry leaves Moseulpo모슬포 Harbor once or twice a day bound for Marado Island. Because the island is so small, it only takes about an hour for a leisurely walk around the island. Surprisingly, there is a chocolate museum (albeit a small one) and a restaurant that sells *jajangmyeon*자장면, Chinese black bean noodles.

Bunjae Artpia

*Bunjae*분재, known as "*bonsai* tree" in Japanese, is considered an art form in the Orient. Bunjae Artpia, the world's largest botanical garden, has trees that are anywhere from 30 to 300 years old. There are maple trees, wisteria, pine trees, plus more than 100 varieties of rare trees.

About 36 years ago, the owner began to create this haven. Despite what others thought about his idea, Sung Beom-young성범영 felt that it was important to go back to nature. His philosophy and spirit can be felt throughout the botanical garden, and one can feel the care and patience that went into all aspects of this labor of love. In many cases, it takes not just years but decades to cultivate a *bunjae*.

The Museum of Sex and Health

Who would have thought that you'd find such an unusual museum hidden on Jejudo? Few Koreans know that such a museum exists on this island. As you enter the museum, the male and female psyche are displayed in several interesting exhibits; the second exhibition hall is reserved for the discovery of the five senses and their impact on sex. This is followed by an exhibition on adolescence, newlyweds, midlife and the senior years, each one outlining different phases of life. There is also an exhibit of sex and numbers, a look at statistics from all around the world. After looking at those displays, you can move on to the sculptures and artifacts from various continents to understand the sexual customs across the ages. There are about 1,200 interesting pieces which are the pride and joy of the museum. The last hall looks at the connection between health and sex: the impact of smoking, drinking on sex, diabetes, hypertension and STDs. At the same time, there are constructive guidelines for having a healthy and happy sex life. There is also an experimental area where visitors can enjoy various activities as well as audiovisual materials.

Haenyeo

"Whee~ whee~" the whistling sound that the *haenyeo* 해녀 make is actually their breathing technique. About 30-40 years ago, when it was difficult to make a living, these women would dive into the sea without any scuba gear whatsoever in order to gather abalone, conch and other shellfish. The lung capacity of these women is astonishing. Since it is such a difficult life and conditions have improved, they no longer have to endure the hardships of diving. Now, they are a dying breed. In the late 1960s, there were about 4,000 *haenyeo*. Currently, there are only about 480 registered *haenyeo*, of which only about 400 are active. The women wear a rubber wetsuit, goggles and lead weights around their waist to take them down 10 meters. Armed with nothing but a hook, they work about 4-5 hours a day. The more experienced dive deep into the sea to cull the more expensive shellfish, while novices stay in the shallower areas to find cheaper shellfish. The average income is about US $50-100 per day.

Traditional Street
Insa-dong

Insa-dong 인사동 is an art and antique district with dozens of art galleries, and shops selling art supplies, antiques, and handicrafts along the main street as well as in small alleys. There are also many traditional tea shops and restaurants that sell traditional Korean food. The best time to visit is on weekends, when the main street is closed to vehicular traffic and you can stroll at a reasonably leisurely pace along the road.

Historically, Insa-dong and the surrounding neighborhood were home to government officials, extended families of royalty and *yangban* 양반 during the Joseon 조선 Dynasty (1392-1910), as it is located near several palaces.

Over 40 percent of all antique stores are found in Insa-dong. Most stores sell old books, pictures and calligraphy, as well as pictures, pottery, wooden containers and jewelry.

Ceramic ware is also a popular item for tourists. It can be used in everyday life but is also appreciated as a decorative item. In April 1999, Queen Elizabeth of England visited the neighborhood, thereby boosting its popularity. The most popular ceramic piece is the gourd-shaped bottle. Be sure that the ceramics you buy have a clear color and a resonant sound when you tap it with your fingernail. Old paintings and calligraphy are also appreciated by visitors. There are many shops which sell old artwork including Oriental paintings. Antique furniture, such as bookshelves and bookstands, as well as stone Buddhas and tiles can also be found.

If you go to Insa-dong on Sundays, when there is no traffic, visit the flea market. You may find a long lost treasure!

[insadong] 인사동

A Traditional Village Nestled in the City
Bukchon

Those who visit Korea for the first time and have never been to Asia might arrive with expectations of an exotic Orient. They are often disappointed to find ultramodern skyscrapers typical of any city in the world. Although Seoul has been the capital of this country for more than 600 years, few historic sites remain other than a few royal palaces here and there. During the rush of economic development, little thought was given to preserving the past.

Right in the heart of downtown Seoul is one place that remains intact, just as it was hundreds of years ago: Bukchon 북촌 literally means "north village" because it is located north of the Cheonggyecheon 청계천 Stream and Jongno 종로, in downtown Seoul. During the Joseon 조선 period, it was an exclusive residential area where high-ranking court officials and nobility lived. It is strategically located between two royal palaces, Gyeongbokgung 경복궁 and Changdeokgung 창덕궁.

Beginning in 1977, earnest efforts were made to preserve this area. Unfortunately, because of random development, only 40 percent of the buildings in the area are *hanok* 한옥, or traditional houses. In 2001, a project was launched to develop the neighborhood as a protected *hanok* village. Most of the 900 extant *hanok* houses date back to the 1920s and 1930s when there was a massive influx of people to the city and subsequent

[bukchon]

urbanization. Today, if you walk around the neighborhood, you can feel how life must have been in the past. If you go in the right direction, you might bump into a jewelry shop, galleries, a workshop specializing in *hanji*한지 (mulberry paper), a small tea shop, lacquerware or a museum dedicated to life in Bukchon. There is also *Haneul Mulbit*하늘물빛, a workshop that produces natural dyes and specializes in the traditional craft of knotting.

A jewel in the heart of Seoul, Bukchon

For those who have never been to Asia, the area might conjure up exotic images and Oriental architecture. In fact, many people are surprised to come to Seoul and see so many modern Western buildings that could place them anywhere in the world.

But nestled in the heart of Seoul is a traditional *hanok* home built in the early 20th century and designated as Historical Site no. 438. This is the house of former President Yun Bo-seon윤보선. The neighborhood in which it is located, Bukchon북촌, between Gyeongbokgung and Changdeokgung Palaces, is actually like a time capsule, with many well-preserved houses. Upon entering former President Yun윤's house, right away you are engulfed by a calm and peacefulness that belies the hustle and bustle of downtown Seoul. Bought by the father of President Yun in 1918, it has been the family residence ever since. Originally 99 *kan*칸 (1 *kan* = 2.4 meters and was the traditional unit to measure houses), it has been greatly reduced in size. Today, the house consists of the women's and men's quarters, a garden, and auxiliary and storage buildings. Though mostly built in the traditional Korean style, Chinese-style brickwork can be seen in the women's quarters and other areas. The interior of the house also reflects Western influence, as can be seen with the tables and chairs there. Interesting to note is the dining table. Commissioned by the president himself, the table blends Western and Korean styles. It is made like a Western table to be used with chairs. However, the corners and finishes are very Korean, like a traditional Korean table, but with longer legs.

The walls are decorated with portraits and photos of the family, one of the most prestigious in Korea.

This home has not only architectural significance, but historically it was the literally cradle of the democratic movement in Korea. The Korea Democratic Party, the first democratic party of Korea, was created here in 1945, and during the 1950s, it was a political beehive, busy with meetings and party activities. The former president used the women's quarters as his office and he even led the anti-autocracy democratic movement as head of the opposition party. The intelligence service even added on a floor to the house opposite in order to keep close tabs on political activities that went on in this house.

A Bustling Business Area
COEX

The Convention and Exhibition Center (COEX) is located in Samseong-dong 삼성동. This stretch is book-ended by two Intercontinental Hotels—the Grand Intercontinental Hotel on one end and the COEX Intercontinental at the other. In between is the convention area as well as a large underground mall where you can eat, shop, enjoy a movie or two, play arcade games or visit the COEX Aquarium.

The high-end Hyundai 현대 Department Store offers many brand names that you would see in other major cities as well as Korean brands. For businessmen, the Trade Tower houses many offices, while the City Air Terminal is convenient for those who want to forget about the hassle of checking in at Incheon International Airport 인천국제공항. They will check your baggage all the way through and so you don't have to worry about it until you reach your destination.

Bongeunsa Temple

If you're too busy to go to the countryside or if you have a few hours to kill between meetings, visit the Bongeunsa 봉은사 Temple, just across the street from the COEX Intercontinental Hotel. You may wonder why the temple is located in such a busy intersection, but the fact is it was built in 794, when the area was completely undeveloped.

If you're lucky, you can catch a meditation session or tea ceremony. The Building of Scriptures stores 3,479 wooden tablets containing 13 types of sutras. Also, under the eaves are wooden name markers written by a great calligraphy master called Kim Jeong-hui 김정희.

[ko-ekseu] 코엑스

Need downtime?
Cheonggyecheon Stream Is the Place to Go

For almost 60 years, the Cheonggyecheon 청계천 Stream was buried under concrete and pavement, with a four-lane elevated motorway built above it. But in September 2005, after two years of construction, the stream saw light again. Cheonggyecheon is a classic case of urban renewal that addresses cultural, physical and environmental issues.

Long ago, this stream was the heart of Seoul, the place where housewives gathered to do laundry and chat, while their children played in the shallow waters. Unfortunately, it later became a neighborhood dump site and an eyesore. During the economic boom years, when development was on everybody's mind, little thought was given to the environment, and in 1971, construction of a 6-km elevated highway was considered a logical part of modernization. The highway seriously impacted the environment and the health of neighborhood residents, however, and heavy traffic raised air pollution to dangerously high levels.

A few years ago, Seoul's mayor initiated a project to restore the Cheonggyecheon Stream to its former glory, with an aim to address both environmental and cultural concerns. The belief was, renewing the stream would also create an aesthetically appealing destination for tourists and investors alike. When the project was first announced, there was a lot of resistance, especially due to anticipated traffic congestion. Driving in Seoul is difficult at best, and eliminating a major artery would mean diverting traffic to other roads which would be further congested. The

청계천 [cheonggyecheon]

shopkeepers were also concerned about their livelihood. Despite the resistance, the project was a success. Property values along the stream have jumped and the stream has inspired new hope.

Today, along the stream you can find marsh-plants and ducks, running tracks, clean waterfalls and a park. There is also a new museum and regular street performances. Historic structures, including the Gwangtonggyo 광통교 and Supyogyo 수표교 Bridges, have been restored.

The Cheonggyecheon Stream has had quite an environmental impact on the surrounding area. The air has become cleaner in Seoul and the temperature is 1-2 degrees lower, even on the hottest days.

The Ugly Duckling Turns into a Swan
Seonyudo Park

Seonyudo 선유도 Park is located off the expressway to Gimpo 김포 International Airport. What is most astonishing about this park is that it used to be a water purification plant. But in 2002, it was transformed into a beautiful park. The ash trees provide welcome shade in the large park; the amphitheater is used for various performances; the aquatic-plant garden is filled with irises and cattails; and the blue bamboo trees, birch trees and moss covering the stone steps are just some of the botanical varieties that you will see. The greenery, however, is just one part of the park's allure. There are buildings and machinery that date back to the defunct water purification plant that was once here. They were left standing as a reminder of the past, but today they blend amazingly well with the greenery.

The highlight of the park has to be the Garden of Green Columns. When the roof of the purification plant was removed, all of the columns were left standing and now they are covered entirely in ivy—Pompeii in a time warp, perhaps. Another impressive sight is the Garden of Time, where the walls, columns and beams of the plant have all been left intact. The space inside, however, has been filled with plants and trees. Seonyudo Park has received numerous awards, including a design award from the American Society of Landscape Architects, the Korean Institute of Architects, the Seoul municipal government and the Kim Soo-gon 김수곤 Culture Award.

선유도 [seonyudo]

A Little Bit of the World in Seoul
Itaewon

What would expats living in Seoul do without Itaewon이태원? This area, which developed as an economic offshoot near America's largest army base, stretches along a 1.4km street. Clothing and bags are mainly in the shopping area closer to the base, while antique furniture and other wares are farther down. Most signs are written in English, and the hawkers and vendors can often communicate in basic English.

People may have difficulty finding clothing elsewhere in the city, but Itaewon has styles and sizes to fit anybody and everybody. Tailors will custom-make dress shirts and suits that are delivered to your hotel the next day. Leather jackets are also a very good buy. Suitcases and various types of bags are in abundance, as are shoes. And for those who like antique furniture, this is the place to buy.

[itaewon] 이태원

Full of Life and Energy
Namdaemun & Dongdaemun Markets

Traditional markets are always full of life and exciting places to visit. Namdaemun 남대문 Market, or South Gate Market is located in the heart of downtown Seoul. The products sold here range from men, women and children's clothing, kitchenware, local and imported goods to eyeglasses and food. Products are sold wholesale and retail, so prices are relatively inexpensive. If you're looking for souvenirs, this is the place to find them. Wholesalers are open from midnight to six in the morning while retailers are open from 7:00 a.m. to 5:00 p.m. If you have a specific store in mind, be sure to check the business hours. The milling crowds make walking around the market a challenge, but the experience is definitely worth it. Street vendors enliven the atmosphere as they shout and clap to attract customers.

Dongdaemun 동대문 Market, or East Gate Market, sells mainly textiles and apparel, both modern and traditional. In fact, if you like Korean traditional clothing, you can have an outfit tailored here at a relatively inexpensive price. Recently, the market has gone through a complete transformation. New buildings offer floors of clothing, and it even has its own website at www.dongdaemun.com. Because many designers are novices trying to break into the fashion business, it is a vibrant and exciting place for young people. If you go in the evening, there are various events, including singing and dance performances. From late night to early morning, buses of visitors and tourists from the countryside and overseas visit Dongdaemun Market. Numerous street stalls offer tasty dishes to satisfy shoppers' hunger. Because it is located next to a large sports stadium, there are also lots of sporting goods for sale.

시장 [sijang]

Home of Seagulls
Dokdo Islets

Located smack in the middle of the East Sea, between Korea and Japan, these rocks have been the center of a heated controversy between the two neighboring countries. Called "Takeshima" in Japanese, the islets are inhospitable but considered valuable for their rich fishing grounds and potential natural gas reserves. Currently only 37 Koreans—police, Ministry of Maritime and Fisheries employees, and one married couple—live there. The islets were recently opened to the public, but because of rough waters, trips are often cancelled, especially in the winter.

Korea claims to have historical records dating back to the sixth century while Japan says its documents go back to the 17th century.

[dokdo]

Experience First-hand the Division of a Country
Panmunjeom

With the fall of the Berlin Wall in 1989, Korea is now the only divided country left in the world. Although the Korean War ended on July 27, 1953, North and South Korea are still technically at war because there is only an armistice agreement in place and not a truce. Following the war, a 2km long demilitarized zone was designated between the two sides. While it has become a tourist destination, it remains a stark reminder of the reality of a divided nation. Often called the 38th parallel, the DMZ cuts the Korean peninsula roughly in half.

The one (and only) beneficial outcome of the DMZ is that while the area is dotted with innumerable landmines, it has become a haven for wildlife. Since humans have been unable to enter this area for more than 50 years, the wildlife has quite literally been able to run wild. Consequently, it has become the most well-preserved piece of temperate land in the world.

What to see
- The 3rd Infiltration Tunnel: a visit to this tunnel really brings home the fact that North Korea still harbors ambitions to attack the South. Kim Bu-seong 김부성, a North Korean defector, led South Korean authorities to the site. The tunnel, which is 2 meters wide and 1,635 meters long, would allow 10,000 armed soldiers to reach Seoul in less than an hour. After it was discovered, the North refused to acknowledge it and instead accused the South of building it to attack the North.

판문점 [panmunjeom]

- Dorasan Observation Platform: when there isn't any fog, it is possible to see the city of Gaeseong개성, North Korea with the naked eye. This observation platform is the northernmost observatory in South Korea.
- There is also a natural spring called *manghyangsu*망향수 or "water of nostalgia" to soothe the broken hearts of those who had to leave their hometowns in the North.
- Bridge of Freedom: so-called because 13,000 war prisoners shouted, "Hurray, Freedom!" when they were released in 1953, thanks to the Armistice Agreement, and returned home over the bridge. Until 1998, it was the only bridge over the Imjingang임진강 River.

The Beauty of 12,000 Mountain Peaks
Geumgangsan

Located in North Korea, the virtually untainted grandeur of the rock face and lovely valleys are truly a sight to see in any season. Many ancient temples and structures on Mt. Geumgangsan 금강산 create a picturesque sight.

Recently, Mt. Geumgangsan was opened to tourists from South Korea. Tourists used to take a cruise to and from Geumgangsan enjoying all the luxuries that a cruise ship offers: a buffet, bar, lounge, gym, theater, shopping mall, club and other facilities. There were also music and magic performances to entertain visitors. But now only overland journey is available. Once they arrive at Mt. Geumgangsan, visitors can choose between four hiking programs which highlight natural formations such as rock cliffs, waterfalls, mountain peaks and valleys.

After the hike, there is a circus performance by the Moranbong 모란봉 circus team, one of the most famous circus troupes in the world. The trip comes to a close with a visit to a relaxing 100% germanium hot spring bath.

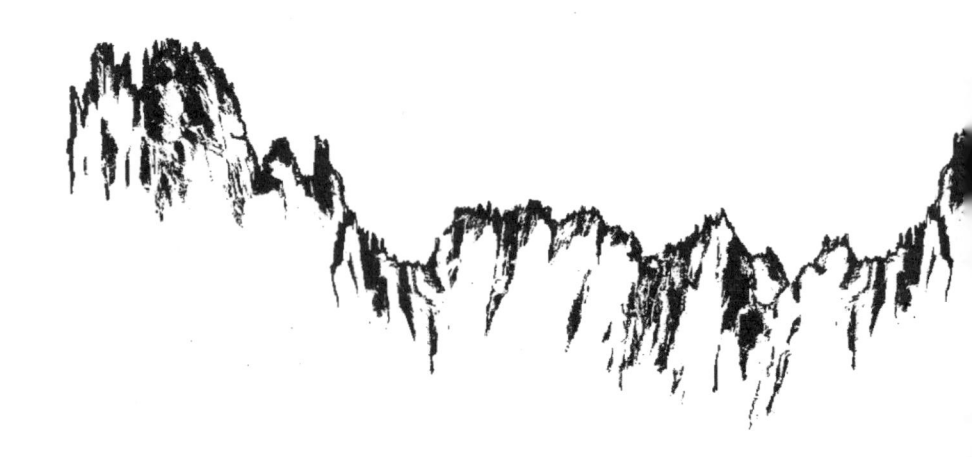

● KOREAN EXPRESSION
금강산 식후경 *geumgangsando sikugyeong*
Even Mt. Geumgangsan can wait until after we eat.

Mt. Geumgangsan has long been considered the most beautiful mountain in Korea. But even its beauty cannot be appreciated on an empty stomach. So, after a long meeting, a Korean might say, *"Geumgangsando sikugyeong* 금강산도 식후경*"* meaning first things first, or no one can work on an empty stomach.

[geumgangsan] 금강산

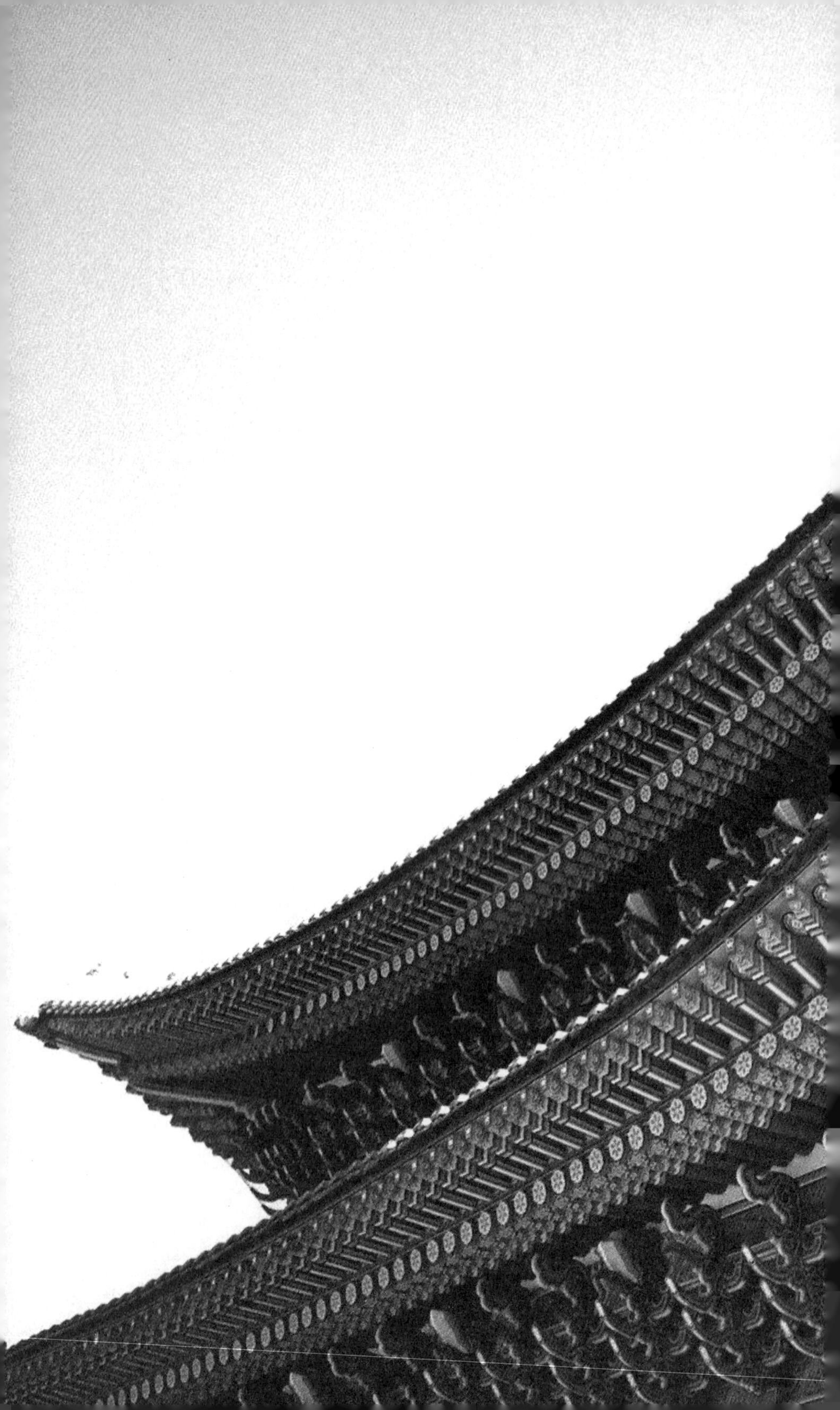

PART 5

Korean Art
: the Beauty of Simplicity

A Reflection of Korean Philosophy
Hanok

Traditionally, the ideal location for a village was facing a river, backed by a mountain. The mountain acted as a wind screen and provided ample firewood while the river supplied drinking water as well as water for farming.

One of the characteristics of Korean housing is the flooring. There are two kinds—the *ondol*온돌 and *maru*마루 systems. The *ondol*, or heated floor, was first developed in the northern regions which experienced long cold winters, while the *maru*, or wooden floor, was ideally suited for the long and humid summers in the south. In today's modern apartments, which are heated by pipes under the floor, bedrooms have heated floors, while living rooms have wooden floors.

To understand the layout of a traditional Korean *yangban*양반 home, it is helpful to know a little bit about Confucianism, which had a deep and lasting influence on all aspects of Korean culture. One of the tenets of Confucianism is that boys and girls over the age of seven must not be together under any circumstances. This also impacted the architecture, and so there were separate living quarters to reflect the separate functions of the men and women in the house. The male quarters were called the *sarangchae*사랑채, consisting of the master *sarangchae* for the father and a junior *sarangchae* for the eldest son. It was the former room that men would meet in. The room was usually slightly elevated so that one would

[hanok] 한옥

have to bow in order to enter. Located adjacent to the kitchen, the *anchae*안채 was where the women and children dwelled. It was ruled by the lady of the house, and was located deep inside the home to restrict the free movement of women. Subsequent rooms for daughter-in-laws, unmarried daughters and sons were all arranged according to their hierarchical positions in the family.

Middle and lower class residences were built in a simple fashion, with rooms, a porch and a kitchen. Unlike upper class homes which had tile roofs, these homes usually had thatched roofs and, depending on the region, oak bark, or pieces of pine. On the southern island of Jejudo제주도, rocks were hung from the roofs to make sure they weren't blown away.

Perhaps because Korea's terrain is quite hilly, curvilinear lines have dominated traditional Korean architecture. The *daecheong maru*대청마루, similar to a Western living room, opened directly to the outside while the curved eaves reached to the skies in a recreation of Korea's natural surroundings.

Korean traditional paper pasted over the wooden-lattice windows and doors was also characteristic of Korean *hanok*. Re-pasting the paper each winter was a chore that had to be finished before the cold weather came. In the past, since weddings were held at the bride's house, the wedding night was spent there as well. The relatives would gather in front of the nuptial room and someone would lick their index finger and then bore a hole in the paper for a peek, much to the laughter and glee of the other relatives. Then, when the groom blew out the candle, the relatives would leave the bride and groom at peace.

An oft-depicted silhouette through the paper is that of a mother pounding the wrinkles out of newly-washed laundry or of a young man studying well into the night.

Traditional Korean paper, *Hanji*

Handmade by processing the bark of the mulberry plant, *hanji*한지 was once the only paper used in Korea. This paper is special because it is made only of natural materials, which means that the paper breathes and therefore, does not change over time. *Hanji* was not only used for keeping historical records, but also for lining doors, walls, and floors. It was also used to record religious ceremonies since the whiteness of the paper symbolized cleanliness and purity.

Today, new uses are being developed. For example, *hanji* is being used to cover lamps, and as a fabric for men's dress shirts and socks. It is surprisingly resilient and versatile.

Nature Untouched
Korean Gardens

For some people, Korea and Japan are often undistinguishable in many ways. However, though the countries are juxtaposed, there are many aspects that differ, from their living environment and way of thinking to their attitude toward culture. The Japanese garden, in particular, is very different from the Korean garden.

The Japanese also revered rocks, and even venerated them as gods because they believed that they linked the world of the gods with men. Japanese gardens are enclosed by a wall inside which mountains, the sea and forests are artificially landscaped. The human hand can be felt not only in the ponds, bridges and man-made constructions, but also in natural objects such as trees. In order to ensure that nature did not get out of hand, most of the trees planted in Japanese gardens were the slow-growing variety.

Why interfere with nature? In a nutshell, that is the general attitude that Koreans had toward their gardens. Thanks to the abundant hills, rocks, trees and water in the environment, the basic elements needed to create a garden already exist. Korean gardens tend to try to preserve nature in its purest form, which is why they are simple and unforced. The foundations of a Korean garden can be found in the ancient tradition of revering nature. The ultimate goal was to make the gardens more natural

정원 [jeong-won]

than nature itself. The gardens are, for the most part, filled with broad-leaf trees, with a few evergreens here and there. Japanese gardens tend to be filled with evergreens because they do not change with the seasons. Yet Koreans wanted to feel the changes in nature and embrace them. Man cannot alter the flow of the seasons but can choose to live in harmony with them.

Beauty in the Lines
Hanbok

The vibrant colors and simple lines of the long, flowing costume worn by women is unique and distinctive to Korea. The women's *hanbok*한복 consists of a long wrap skirt that is tied above the breasts and a short vest. The men's pants are roomy and are accompanied by a shirt, vest and outer jacket. There are no zippers or buttons—ribbons are used to tie or close any part of the garment.

The *hanbok*, which dates back to the Three Kingdoms era (BC 57-AD 676), made it possible to tell the social standing of a person simply by looking at how they were dressed. Commoners wore white unadorned *hanbok* and were allowed to wear a different color only on special occasions. Courtiers had different symbols and emblems embroidered on their belts to indicate their standing. The *yangban*양반 (aristocracy) wore *hanbok* made of woven ramie cloth in warm weather and silk during the rest of the year.

Today it is worn on special occasions, and those for weddings or special birthdays can be quite expensive since they are usually made of silk.

Up until the end of the Joseon 조선 Dynasty, it was unthinkable to cut one's hair because it was a gift given by one's parents. Boys and girls alike would braid their hair until they were married. Then the men would wear their hair up in a *sangtu*상투 (topknot) which was covered at all times

한복 [hanbok]

except in the privacy of one's home, and the women wore their hair in a bun at the nape of their neck. "Letting one's hair down" was something that Koreans did only at home!

Visual Art Expressed
Through Lines

While Western art tends to emphasize forms and color, Korean art focuses on lines and empty space. Lines are bold and striking while the colors are both complex and refined, all of which harmonizes well.

Korean calligraphers not only consider Chinese characters to be an art, but more recently, they also see hangeul한글 (Korean alphabet) as an art form as well. Even the Chinese themselves recognized that calligraphy combined with handmade hanji한지 (Korean paper) created an art in itself.

Buddhist statues, which are commonplace in temples scattered throughout Japan, are actually masterpieces of Korean sculpture. Historically, there are many Buddhist statues of the style produced in the Horiyuji era in Japan that were made by Korean sculptors. Korean sculptures do not have the exaggerated features of Chinese art, nor are they grandiose. Rather, the lines and proportions portray complex emotions, simplicity and restraint, which were considered virtues.

Folk paintings

Folk paintings were realistic depictions of the lives of commoners, sometimes with a touch of humor. The themes included nature, and among animal themes, tigers and crows were favorites. There is nothing arrogant about these folk paintings; rather, they depict the down-to-earth feelings of common people.

Another trend was that of the aristocratic officials who blindly followed Chinese techniques. Their subjects were mainly apricot blossoms, chrysanthemums, orchids, bamboo, mountains and rivers. Because longevity was highly valued, plants and animals which symbolized longevity were often drawn.

전통미술 [jeontong misul]

Where Art and Practicality Meet
Pottery

Records indicate that clay was first used on the Korean peninsula during the Neolithic era. By the Three Kingdoms era (BC 57-AD 676) earthenware was in common use around the peninsula. It was during the Unified Silla 통일신라 era (676-935) that the shapes and decorative patterns became more diverse.

During the Goryeo 고려 era (918-1392), ceramic ware was developed and appreciated for its greater durability and impermeability. The Goryeo era brought about the world-renowned *cheongja* 청자, a ceramic with a clear, pale green hue. The inlaid intricate designs were prized for their beauty and artistic flair. The green hue was produced by adding iron to the glaze and because it replicated the color of jade, which was considered precious at the time, it was greatly appreciated. The most popular motifs were cranes, clouds, ponds and trees.

During the Joseon 조선 era (1392-1910), *baekja* 백자 gained a foothold. *Baekja* pieces were much simpler than *cheongja*. While *cheongja* mirrored aristocratic culture and luxuries, *baekja* reflected Joseon era aristocratic scholars who prized a noble mind and humility above all other virtues. The motifs used during this era were mainly dragons, pine trees, cranes and peonies. The pottery-making techniques that were passed on to Japan were from this era.

Today, if you visit the Icheon 이천 Ceramics Festival, you can make your own work of art just like the potters of yore, or simply watch to see how it is done.

[dojagi] 도자기

Korean Traditional Music

Korean traditional music used to be divided into music for the ruling class and that for the common people. Music for the upper class consisted of ensemble-type music, lyric songs, indigenous popular songs as well as music related to Confucian rituals. Such music is very sedate and to Western ears might sound almost static. In some cases, a beat can even last three seconds. The instruments are made of non-metallic materials. String instruments are made of silk rather than wire, and almost all the wind instruments are made of bamboo, which adds to their special aura.

Music for commoners, which includes shaman music, Buddhist music, folk songs, farmers' music and *pansori*판소리, is much easier for most people to enjoy. In shaman music, the female shaman priest acts as a medium between the present world and the supernatural, and one of the means to communicate is through music. *Beompae*범패 is a song of praise to Buddha that has been passed on through generations of monks. It has been designated as an Intangible Cultural Property in order to preserve it.

Farmers' music is indispensable to celebrate the different points in the agricultural season. In *pansori*, which can be marathon performances lasting more than eight hours, the singer delivers enthralling ballads in a unique style, accompanied by only one musician.

Traditional Korean music is characterized by improvisation and the lack of breaks between movements. It is also marked by a pace that begins with the slowest movement and then picks up and the performance continues. There are more than 60 different traditional instruments. Here are a few examples of the ones used most widely.

Pansori, Korean opera

Dating back to the mid-Joseon조선 era (1392-1910), *pansori* is quite simple. It consists of a singer, the *sorikkun*소리꾼, and a drummer, the *gosu*고수. In good storytelling tradition, the singer sings the story while the drummer accompanies by providing the beat and shouting words of encouragement to add to the passion of the performance. Because it is such an exhausting performance for the singer, only the fittest manage to survive the rigors demanded. It is said that a true *pansori* singer is able to sing overtop the sound of a waterfall.

In 2003, UNESCO officially recognized *pansori* as an important part of world culture.

[jeontong eumak]

Traditional Korean Instruments

Wind instruments

Piri 피리
Piri is a cylindrical oboe. It has a long, wide double reed and eight finger holes, including the back thumb hole. It is the leading instrument and always takes the main melody in Korean court music or folk ensembles. Its sound is loud and has a distinctive tone quality and timbre.

Taepyeongso 태평소
Taepyeongso, literally "great peace flute," is a conical wooden oboe with eight finger holes, a metal mouthpiece, and a cup-shaped metal bell. It produces a loud and piercing sound and is used for farmers' band music, traditional military band music and some folk music.

String instruments

Geomungo 거문고
Geomungo is representative of zithers with six strings of twisted silk. The strings are plucked with a bamboo rod which is held between the index and middle fingers of the right hand, while the left hand presses on the strings to produce microtones.

Gayageum 가야금
Gayageum, which can be traced back to the sixth century, is another type of Korean zither, with 12 silk strings supported by 12 movable bridges. The thumb, index and middle fingers of the right hand pluck the strings, while the index and middle fingers of the left hand touch the strings on the left side of the movable bridges. The tone quality is clear and delicate.

Percussion instruments

Kkwaenggwari 꽹과리
Used mainly in farmers' music and shaman music, *kkwaenggwari* leads rhythmic patterns when it is struck with a wooden mallet, producing a sharp sound that commands attention. It is the smallest of the gongs and is hand-held.

Janggo 장고
Janggo, or hourglass drum, is the most frequently used accompaniment in almost all forms of Korean music. The thick skin of the left side is struck with the palm and produces a soft, low sound. The thin skin of the right side is struck with a bamboo stick to produce a hard, crisp sound. The pitch of the right side can be made higher or lower by tightening or loosening the tension of the drum head. This is done by moving the central belts encircling the V-shaped laces to the right or to the left.

Pyeongyeong 편경
Pyeongyeong is a set of 16 L-shaped slabs of jade stone. The counterpart of bell chimes, it has played an essential role in court ceremonies since the 12th century. The stone slabs are all of the same size and shape but vary in thickness so that each has a different pitch. The thickest produces the highest pitch while the thinnest one produces the lowest.

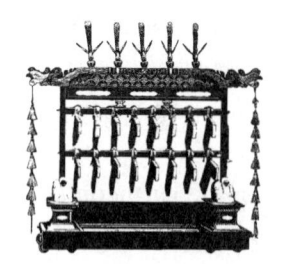

Korean Musicals in Disguise
Masks and Mask Dances

Dating back to prehistoric times, masks and mask dances in Korea can be categorized into religious masks and artistic masks. Some religious masks were revered with offerings, while other religious masks were used to expel evil spirits, such as during funeral processions. Artistic masks were used in dance and drama.

Korean masks have a black cloth to cover the back of the head, which anchors the mask and also simulates black hair. The masks were used not only to depict the character's role but also to mirror the expressions and bone structure of Koreans. However, because the mask dance was often performed at night, illuminated only by campfires or candle light, the masks were exaggerated and grotesque, with bright, vivid colors. In contrast, masks used during the daytime and religious masks were less exaggerated. The red, black, white and other primary colors indicated the gender and age of the characters. For example, black was used for an old person, red for a young man and white for a young woman. Furthermore, colors were also identified with directions and seasons. For example, black stood for the north and winter, and red for the south and summer.

Since the mask dance was an expression of the trials and tribulations of commoners, they portrayed their hostile feelings toward the *yangban* 양반 (aristocrat) by distorting the facial features. Masks were always deformed

달과 탈춤 [talgwa talchum]

with harelips, cleaved lips, lopsided mouths, distorted noses or squinty eyes. Depending on the region, the masks and stories vary somewhat, but they all had the same fundamental elements, ranging from exorcism rites and ritual dances to parodies of human weaknesses and the social and privileged class.

All the actors in a mask dance performance used to be male, but that changed when *gisaeng*기생, or female entertainers, began to play the role of shamans and concubines. The mask dance involves a mixture of dialog, delivered in a greatly exaggerated manner, and pantomime. What is most entertaining about the mask dance is that the performers are very interactive with the audience who can chime in to encourage, criticize or warn the actors at any time. By the end of the performance, the actors and audience alike join in a merry dance.

Grace in Motion
Traditional Dance

Traditional dances can be divided into court dances and folk dances. Since the court dances aimed to glorify the court and pray for a long life for the king, they were invariably solemn and accentuated by elegant choreography. To some, however, it might appear as a lack of movement. The restraint in the dance movements were due to Confucianist influence. To offset the serene movements, the stage settings and costumes were dramatic and opulent. Depending on the theme and role of the dance, there were different garments, shoes and extended sleeves, in particular. The main colors (red, blue, yellow, white and black) were used to coincide with the five cardinal elements of the cosmos.

Folk dances were easy to understand because they were based on the everyday lives of the commoners. Though styles differ according to region, they all depict festive occasions and community rituals. As in other countries, folk dances originated in prayers for a good harvest, or in some cases, were forms of entertainment. With simple plots, the themes are universal and can easily be understood by everybody, even today.

전통춤 [jeontong chum]

Salpuri 살풀이, the spirit-cleansing dance
Shamanism first appeared in Korea around the Three Kingdoms era. A shaman (*mudang* 무당) presided over the entire process, with *salpuri* being the culmination of the shaman ritual. Though the *salpuri* has its roots in shamanistic ritual, it has evolved over the centuries to become a true artistic performance. The dancer enters a trance-like state and throws herself into energetic movements. To add to the drama, the dance begins with a slow tempo and gradually builds up speed. Most noticeable is the shaman's rhythmic jumping motions, almost like audiences at a rock concert.

Seungmu 승무, the monk dance
A dancer dressed like a monk in grey robes with long white sleeves dances alone, blending flowing movements with abrupt bursts of stillness. Designated as Intangible Cultural Property No. 27, it is based in Buddhist ceremonial dances and was considered an essential dance in the repertoire of any true dancer for many years.

Forget Your Troubles in
Traditional Games

Koreans have always loved various games and competitions. There were one-on-one competitions like *ssireum* 씨름 (Korean wrestling) which involved sheer strength, as well as group competitions accompanied by vibrant music. Such pastimes helped to wash away the fatigue of the farmers as well as create an atmosphere of cooperation. The following are a few traditional games that Koreans have enjoyed.

Chajeon nori 차전놀이 (Juggnaut battle): *Chajeon nori* is called a game but it actually involves the entire village or community. Two "ships" are made from wood and old rice stalks. The leader stands at the top of the ship while the others hold it. The two east and west ships ram into each other until one of the leaders falls down or the ship touches the ground. Accompanied with traditional music, it is a battle of wills and pride.

Jultagi 줄타기 (Rope walking): Not "played" by ordinary people, it was a spectacle that one could see when markets would open. The rope walker doesn't just walk on the rope, but jumps up and down, turns around and does other acrobatic feats that are dangerous, considering there is no safety net.

Yeon nalligi 연날리기 (Kite flying): It is not just for children. On major holidays such as Lunar New Year's Day 설날 and Chuseok 추석, it is easy to spot kites flying high in the sky. The traditional Korean kite is made with bamboo sticks and rice paper and is usually rectangular.

Neolttwigi 널뛰기 (Korean see-saw): Instead of sitting on either side, the traditional Korean see-saw involves standing at each end and jumping. It is usually enjoyed by females during traditional holidays and festivals. The object is to try to jump as high as possible.

Paengi chigi 팽이치기 (Spinning tops): Korean tops are made of wood, with a string wrapped around the bottom, that is yanked to get the top spinning. The object is to have your top spin the longest or in other games to kick your opponent's top out of the game. The string can also be used to whip the top so that it spins longer. Tops are enjoyed mostly by boys.

Jegi chagi 제기차기 (Kicking the *jegi*): The *jegi* 제기 resembles a shuttlecock, and was traditionally kicked around by boys. The object was to keep it from hitting the ground and to perform as many fancy moves as possible.

[nori munhwa] 놀이문화

Ssireum 씨름 (Korean wrestling): There are some similarities between Korean wrestling and Japanese *sumo* wrestling. *Ssireum* is conducted in a small ring filled with sand and the wrestlers are quite hefty. Yet unlike *sumo* wrestling, *ssireum* has different weight categories and involves more body to body contact. While *sumo* wrestlers simply try to push each other out of the ring, the objective of *ssireum* is to get your opponent on the ground while staying within the ring. There are many different techniques that involve a great deal of skill.

Baduk 바둑 (Go): Better known in the West by its Japanese name, "go," *baduk* is a game of strategy that is played by two people on a grid. One player has black pawns, the other white. The objective is to surround your opponent's pawns in order to occupy the territory.

A very popular game in Korea, if you go to any public park today you are sure to see grandfathers playing *baduk*. There is a *baduk* cable channel and there are also different championships with a hefty sum of prize money. *Baduk* champions are well-known in Korea.

Janggi 장기 (Korean board game): This Korean board game is very similar to Western chess, but the playing board, pieces and rules are slightly different. A chess player would have no trouble adjusting. The main difference is that the pieces have Chinese characters written on them.

The Way of Fist and Feet
Taekwondo

If China has kung fu and Japan has karate, Korea has taekwondo 태권도. An official Olympic sport since the 2000 Sydney Olympic Games, taekwondo has truly been the sports ambassador for Korea, making more people aware of this country than any other product or event.

Taekwondo is a compound word which literally means "to kick or destroy with the foot," "fist" and "art." Therefore, taekwondo is the art of destroying with feet and fists. Taekwondo blends together combat techniques, self-defense, sport and exercise alongside an underlying philosophy of self-discipline.

The aim of taekwondo lies in training the body and mind through disciplines: precise judgment and confidence along with strong physical strength and willpower becoming strong to the strong, and gentle to the weak; and cultivating one's own virtue in a courteous manner rather than trying to defeat an enemy. That is why many parents send their kids to taekwondo in Korea. It is not a traditional sport that they simply enjoy watching, but a friendly sport that compliments one's daily life.

Taekwondo is now popular around the world as an international sport. No matter where you are, it is not difficult to find somewhere to learn taekwondo. There are currently about 50 million people learning or interested in taekwondo in countries around the world, and that number is only increasing.

[taekwondo] 태권도

Jump!

This is an exciting and unique non-verbal performance that blends taekwondo and other traditional Korean martial arts. It can be seen at its exclusive theater from September 1, 2006, or you can pay a visit to its website at www.yegam.com/jump/kor.

> *Jump!* was shown at the Edinburgh Fringe Festival and
> at Sadler's Wells theater in West End in London to rave reviews.
> _Five stars by the 《British Theatre Guide》

"This is probably the most exhilarating 'family show' I've ever seen. It is literally about a Korean family, grandpa, mum and dad, teenager son (a bit of a boozer), pretty teenage daughter and the guest who arrives to woo her. Grandpa is a bit authoritarian and puts the family through their paces, martial arts paces that is, and we are treated to a display of the athletic talents that make the grand progenitor proud. The daughter's suitor is a bit of a dark horse too. Seemingly a myopic wimp, when his thick, ugly glasses are removed, he goes through a shuddering transformation into a lusty Jet Li.

The plot thickens when a couple of burglars break into the house in the middle of the night; one a sleek, mean villain, the other a plump dimwit with scarey hair. When the family discovers the intruders a mighty battle ensues which takes just about every possible comic twist in the book and a host of new ones to boot, including shooting the stage manager. This is slapstick like you've never seen it before, with sight gags lifted onto another plane through martial arts, acrobatics and sword play.

There is also some parody of the Kung Fu and Wu Xi films that is highly entertaining. The sheer dynamism of this company makes the spirits soar. It is invigorating stuff from a cast of considerable generosity. Not only are their acrobatic feats impressive, but they are cultural ambassadors, reminding us appropriately at an international festival that laughter transcends specifics of cultural and nationality.

Go and see this show and take all your family and friends, too.
They will love you forever."
_Jackie Fletcher

"They're not just dazzling acrobats, they're blessed with remarkable come timing they literally don't put a foot wrong."
_《The Scotsman》

"Did I give it five stars? Make it 50."
_《The Evening Standard》

PART 6

Meet
Korea Today
: Everthing Changes
Except Change Itself

At the Cutting Edge
IT Korea

As of the end of 2004, Korea has, for four years running, led the broadband penetration rate, with 24.9 people out of 100 connected to the Internet, followed by the Netherlands at 19. The only other Asian country to place in the top ten was Japan, while the US ranked 12th.

OECD Broadband Subscribers Per 100 Residents
(as of the end of 2004)

RANK	NATION	SUBSCRIBERS
1	Korea	24.9
2	Netherlands	19.0
3	Denmark	18.8
4	Iceland	18.3
5	Canada	17.8
6	Switzerland	17.3
7	Belgium	15.6
8	Japan	15.0
9	Finland	15.0
10	Norway	14.9

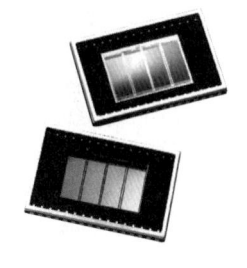

Source: OECD

The reason Korea was able to become an Internet powerhouse was because it makes vast investments in asymmetric digital subscriber lines (ADSL), which are indispensable for pumping data at breakneck speeds.

[cheomdan han-guk] 첨단한국

IT in Korea in a nutshell

- Average monthly Internet use per person is 1,340 minutes.
- 1/8 of the population has signed up for Cyworld.
- Emergence of webocracy (web+democracy) — Roh Moo-hyun 노무현, the first president in the world to be elected by the Internet.
- 71% of the entire population uses the Internet — high acceptance levels of new technology.
- Spread of digitalization, such as future-oriented home networks which link the Internet with household appliances and online games.
- Improvements in education system — free classes provided on the Internet for students preparing for college entrance exams.
- 10% of the economically active population is involved in the IT industry.
- Boosted by outstanding infrastructure and proactive R&D, one out of every five cell phones in the world is "Made in Korea."
- The daily lives of Korean teenagers revolve around mobile devices.
- SMS messages are sent and received 45 times a day.
- 15% of teenagers play mobile games every day.
- Korea leads the world in mobile banking: Internet banking including transactions through mobile handsets overtook bank teller transactions in September 2005; Internet-based transactions constitute 30.9% of total financial transactions; mobile banking more than doubles each year, 104.4% growth each year.
- Mobile broadcasting and broadband Internet service: world's first DMB launched in December 2005 and WiBro services in June 2006.
- State-of-the-art broadband network infrastructure meets market needs such as popularity of Internet games — 12 million high-speed Internet subscribers and 22,000 Internet cafes.
- According to KITA(Korea International Trade Association), semiconductors accounted for 10% of total exports, mobile devices 9.9% and computers 7.9% — out of the top five exports. The other exports were ships 10% and cars 8.1%.

- IT industry accounts for 12.1% of GDP (2004).
- As of 2005, Korea ranks first in IT competitiveness among OECD countries, more than double the OECD average.
- Developed world's first 16G NAND flash memory; world's first trial service of WiBro during APEC 2005 and Torino Olympics; Korea's IT companies received the most CES innovative awards, three years running (2004-2006).
- Smart users lead Korea's IT market: Korean subscribers are willing to pay for high-end devices and subscribe to new IT services.

Cell phone changing cycle

COUNTRY	UNITS/MONTH
Korea	12
USA	21
Canada	30
Russia	24
Poland	24

Korean Culture Sweeping Across Asia
Hallyu

The first golden age of Korean cinema was in the late 1950s and 1960s. Domestic film production increased and the public came to the theaters in large numbers. However, when President Park Chung-hee 박정희 took over, the government began censoring all aspects of the industry, which stifled creative development.

In the 1970s, the public turned to television and remained glued to it for a long time. The first glimmer of change was when Kang Soo-yeon 강수연 received the Best Actress Award in 1987 at the Venice Film Festival for her performance in *Surrogate Mother*.

The director that made his name during the 1980s was Im Kwon-taek 임권택 who dealt with very Korean themes such as Buddhism in Korean society. In 1993, *Seopyeonje* 서편제 which featured *pansori* 판소리 (see page 164), brought about a revival of this art form.

At about the time of the 1988 Olympic Games in Seoul, there were two major changes. First, the film industry saw a gradual easing of censorship laws. Second, import restrictions on foreign films were lifted and Hollywood companies could set up offices in Korea. This meant that Korean films had to compete directly with Hollywood movies. Since they had been on a downhill slide for more than two decades, domestic films saw their market share slipping away until reaching their lowest point in 1993 at 16%. Thanks to the screen quota system, which made it

한류 [hallyu]

mandatory to screen Korean movies for 106-146 days of the year, the domestic film industry was saved.

In 1992, *Marriage Story*, a light sex comedy, was a turning point in many ways. It was not only a different genre which gained critical and popular reviews, but the movie was made by Samsung 삼성, the first major Korean conglomerate to enter the film industry, meaning that financing would become less problematic for filmmakers.

Various directors soon became household names with original and creative films. In 1999, *Shiri* 쉬리 met with unprecedented box-office success, marking the beginning of the second golden era of Korean film.

Internationally, Korean films have won numerous awards at Cannes, Berlin, Venice and other international film festivals. Domestically, they have enjoyed box-office success, too. By 2001, the 60-70 Korean films made each year were more popular than the 200-300 Hollywood and foreign films released on the domestic market.

Korean films are not only enjoying popularity on their home ground, but they are also popular across Asia and Europe. Especially in Asia, Korean films are part of *hallyu* 한류 (Korean wave), the popular spread of Korean culture encompassing TV shows and songs. At first, Korean shows were broadcast in other Asian countries because they were relatively inexpensive compared to American ones. But as exposure increased, there was a groundswell because these TV shows resonated with Asian audiences. The closer cultural affinity has probably helped—the actors look similar and the values portrayed in the dramas are similar—mainly family issues, love and filial piety.

Thanks to *hallyu*, the Korean wave of popular culture sweeping across Asia, interest in the Korean language, food and traditions has increased. Tourism has also been positively affected with fans visiting the locations where *Winter Sonata* 겨울연가, *Jewel in the Palace* 대장금 and other TV shows were shot.

Fast and Efficient Transportation System

You might think that without Korean language skills, you'd have difficulty getting around Korea's major cities. However, in Seoul, Busan, Incheon, and other major cities, the subway system spreads out like a spider web, making it convenient to travel all over. Seoul's first subway started running in 1974 and today there are nine subway lines. You don't have to know Korean because all the names of the stations are also written in English. The most recent addition to Korea's modern transportation system is the KTX, or Korea Train Express. Based on France's TGV—high speed train—technology, Korea also has developed a high speed train network with trains traveling at more than 200km/h. Linking Seoul, Daejeon, Daegu and Busan—Korea's major cities—the KTX shortened travel from Seoul to Busan from 260 minutes to 160 minutes. It is now possible to live outside the city and commute to Seoul.

[gyotong] 교통

Korea's Room Culture

Beginning in the 1990s, the so-called *bang*방, or room culture, became an irreversible trend. The first to gain popularity was the *noraebang*노래방, or singing rooms. Since Koreans love to belt out tunes, especially after they've had a drink or two, this was a natural phenomenon. Everybody's a star at a *noraebang*. For about $15, you rent a room with TV screens and preprogrammed songs which you choose to sing. The *noraebang* was soon followed by video-*bang* and DVD-*bang*, but most notably, by the game-*bang*, or game rooms, which became popular thanks to the on-line game StarCraft.

Released in April 1998 in the US, StarCraft has sold more than three million copies worldwide. Often called the greatest game of the 20th century, more than 700,000 copies have been sold in Korea, and it is estimated that more than two million people enjoy the game. Its explosive popularity has had a ripple effect across society. More than anything, it has led to the formation of game rooms, which have gained a foothold as a veritable industry. Until early 1998, there were only about a hundred or so game rooms with Internet access, but with the lightspeed popularity of StarCraft, the number mushroomed to 8,000.

In the process, the computer and Internet cable industry had an unexpected windfall. With an average of 30 computers per game room, computer companies sold, conservatively, about 240,000 PCs. Companies that specialized in laying Internet lines had faced chronic deficits, but as of 1998, they started moving into the black. When one considers that most game rooms operate around the clock and each employee works an

게임방 [geimbang]

eight-hour shift, 24,000 new jobs have been created.

In a year's time, the economic impact of these game rooms reached two trillion won. The initial investment for these 8,000 game rooms—buying the PCs, software, etc.—was said to be around 100 million won. That alone created 800 billion won.

When one considers that this all occurred during the 1997 Asian financial crisis, it is no exaggeration to say that the game industry breathed new life into the Korean economy.

Progamers

Boosted by the explosive popularity of StarCraft, a new profession, the progamer, has been created. Currently, there are about a dozen recognized progamers who make a living on their winnings from contests, in Korea. Earning a yearly average income of 100 million won, these progamers are considered idols to their game fans.

There are two major game channels, Ongamenet and MBC Game which are viewed by millions of fans. From 2002, SK Telecom and KTF started to sponsor progamers.

Room culture

Why is it that Koreans are so partial to the "room culture"? This is most likely because a closed space offers comfort and security. Within this personal space, you can avoid the stares (or glares) of strangers and find your own pleasure. Inside this enclosed space, you can scream to your heart's content, watch a racy video or tell dirty jokes on the phone. In a word, it is a release from political, economic and social pressures.

While PC rooms began with the "healthy" intention of providing high speed information access and downloads, these Internet cafes had trouble making ends meet. In the meantime, game rooms, which were used for network gaming and accessing pornographic sites, experienced an unprecedented boom precisely because they provided a form of release.

A World Inside the Internet
Cyworld

Today, three out of four Korean teenagers have a computer and are hooked on Cyworld and Kart Rider, the main drivers of Korean IT cultural contents. What's Cyworld? Cyworld is a mini-homepage that exists on the Internet, a place you can meet friends and create your own cyberworld. If you want to converse with kids in Korea today, you have to have a "Cyworld hompy." Short for "cyber world," Cyworld is a Web community site which consists of operating a hompy (short for "home page") and cultivating on and off-line relationships by forming buddy relationships. You can decorate your minihompy however you like—with photos, a message board, guestbooks and a personal bulletin board. While about 25 percent of the population of Korea is said to be registered users, it is estimated that 90% of South Koreans in their 20s have a minihompy.

Unlike other blog sites, Cyworld has a "miniroom," a virtual room where the user creates an avatar, or "mini-me." In order to decorate the room and avatar, users buy "acorns," the currency in Cyworld.

Cyworld is so popular because of its simplicity. Much like shopping off-line, buying items to decorate your minihompy is not so daunting. "Cyworld takes up a lot of my time, but I enjoy uploading my photos and my thoughts and really making it my own personal space. It is my link to other people," said a college student. It is equated to a one-person media outlet and is an effective tool to bring people closer together. With a click of a button, you can keep tabs on past friends. If friends or family go abroad, you can still keep in touch with them.

싸이월드 [ssai woldeu]

Cyworld is also creating another *hallyu*한류. Since some of the functions have been localized to suit local needs, the number of Chinese and Japanese subscribers to Cyworld is increasing, and Kart Rider, called popkart in Chinese, is also gaining popularity. Kart Rider is an on-line game with 3D technology and cute characters. In a word, it is a user-friendly car racing game.

Currently about 50,000 new subscribers log on to Kart Rider and spend about an average of two hours playing the game. Among online games, it continues to break records for simultaneous connections.

Though it is enjoyed mainly by teenagers, it can be enjoyed by the entire family. If you want to find out if someone is a registered Cyworld user, all you have to know is their name and age. As our lives become more complicated and busier, it is difficult to find the time to meet everybody, but cyberspace has become a virtual social gathering place. Friends you've lost touch with for several years can be found again; you can keep in touch with friends and relatives living far away; and you can also find your first love.

Becoming addicted to Cyworld

Cyworld has even produced a different language. *Ssaijilhada*싸이질하다 is a derogatory word for "doing Cy." The reason for this neologism is that once you get into it, it can be very addictive. If somebody pays your minihompy a visit, it is good manners to reciprocate — if you don't, they will not come back, and it is imperative to keep the number of visits rising. In order to attract more visits, you have to invest more time in constantly refurbishing your minihompy with new pictures and new décor.

Early Adopters

It seems that every day new MP3s, cell phones, digital cameras and other small gadgets are being released with new functions that you never knew you needed before! In Korea, interest in such gadgets is far greater than in other countries.

In Korea, groups of "early adopters" with the inclination toward becoming "prosumers"—those who influence manufacturing companies and are actively involved in the improvement of products—have appeared. Even in Japan, where the mania-like propensity to consume products is at the same level as in Korea, early adopters, or "prosumers," that are involved in companies' production process are still unfamiliar idea. It is no exaggeration to say that Korean consumers (prosumerse) are the most advanced in the world. What sets them apart has to do with the characteristics of Korean people as a whole, people who are good at collective behavior, as well as Koreans' active use of the Internet.

International companies have recognized that Koreans are "early adopters" and therefore use Korea as a test bed to judge the reaction of consumers. If it succeeds in Korea, it'll succeed in the rest of the world.

"Keeping up with the Joneses" is a big thing in Korea; fads come and go quickly. And while in the past, large, relatively cheap home electronics were popular exports, today, Korean portable electronic goods with innovative designs are conquering world markets.

얼리어답터 [eolli eodapteo]

B-boys on Top of the World

B-boy, or break boy, was picked up in Korea in 1980, and today Korean B-boys have become world-class dancers, sweeping numerous international contests. Together with Korean movies and TV shows, B-boys have become the new thing in *hallyu*한류. In fact, many tours include B-boy performances which are breathtaking in their intricate and dynamic moves. Each moment is an amazing blending of music and movements. B-boys are a natural correlation with Koreans' natural love for music and dance, passion, as well as the determination to see things through to the end. Though it was started in the West, this dance has transformed into a new cultural code that Korea is riding on to reach out to the West.

B-boy teams battle for 15 minutes when they are giving impromptu music, during which time they must prove their acrobatic prowess and techniques that push the envelope in physical flexibility and power. In order to do one better than their opponents, they must have a good strategy and player arrangement. It is important not only to have the basic moves down pat, but also to add a little extra that makes a move "mine." Some of the moves include head spins, handstands, a flare similar to a gymnast spinning on the pommel horse, and a windmill spinning on the shoulders and chest while keeping the legs off the floor. By winning the Battle of the Year competition in Germany in 2002, 2004 and 2005, the

[biboi] 비보이

UK's B-boy Championship and the US's Free Style Session, Korean B-boys have dominated international competitions, and they have been invited to perform at the opening ceremony of the 2008 Beijing Olympics.

B-boys have become so popular that they are the topic of TV soap operas, comic book series and also movies. Cable channels also broadcast B-boy competitions live and an exclusive B-boy theater has been built near Hong-ik University in Seoul.

CHOI Jung-wha

Professor at the Graduate School of Interpretation and Translation, Hankuk University of Foreign Studies in Korea, she was the first Korean to receive a conference interpretation diploma (Korean, French, English). Currently as president of the Corea Image Communication Institute, she manages the Korea CQ forum which aims to promote a positive image of Korea. She is also a member of the National Image Promotion Board.

She received major awards including the Palme Académique and Legion d'Honneur from the French government for her contribution to education, communication and cultural exchange as well as the Prix Danica Seleskovitch from the Association of Danica. She also authored numerous books including *Interpretation, Translation and Foreign Languages, Dare to Become an Interpreter, Teaching Foreign Languages to Children, English Expressions Most Misunderstood by Koreans*.

LIM Hyang-ok

Currently professor at the Graduate School of Interpretation and Translation, Hankuk University of Foreign Studies in Korea, she also has interpreted for innumerable conferences including summit meetings such as APEC, ASEAN+3 and UN General Assembly meetings. She is a member of AIIC (Association Internationale des Interpretes de Conference) since 1995. She also acts as a communications consultant providing tailor-made English communication and English language programs. She has also written *English for International Conferences* and *Use the Right Word*.

Photo Credits
* Jae-sik Suh
  pp. 26, 117, 146, 147, 149, 162, 179, 191
* Institute of Traditional Korean Food
  pp. 89, 100, 102, 104, 106, 107, 109